THE VENETIANS

POLAND

EUROPE

ARY

ROMANIA

Don River

Tana

RUSSIA

CAUCASUS
MOUNTAINS

CRIMEA

BLACK SEA

BULGARIA

Danube River

CONSTANTINOPLE

Trebizond

Adrianople
THRACE

Bosporus

ARMENIA

Scutari

Gallipoli

Sea of Marmara

TURKEY

GREECE

*Hellespont
(Dardanelles)*

Tenedos

Mytilene

*AEGEAN
SEA*

ANATOLIA (ASIA MINOR)

SEA

CORFU

Cape Santa Maria

*IONIAN
SEA*

*Gulf
of
Arta*

Negroponte

Chios

Cape
Colonne

Lepanto

*Gulf of Lepanto
(Gulf of Corinth)*

Cape Papas

THE

Myra

SYRIA

Zante PELOPONNESUS

RHODES

Nicosia

Famagusta

Zonchio

CYPRUS

Modon

Sapientza

Tripoli

Cape
Matapan

CRETE

Beirut

Sidon

Damascus

Tyre

Acre

Haifa

Jaffa

Jerusalem

HOLY LAND

Ascalon

Alexandria

Suez

EGYPT

Nile River

RED SEA

The Seafarers · THE VENETIANS

Other Publications:

THE EPIC OF FLIGHT
THE GOOD COOK
THE ENCYCLOPEDIA OF COLLECTIBLES
THE GREAT CITIES
WORLD WAR II
HOME REPAIR AND IMPROVEMENT
THE WORLD'S WILD PLACES
THE TIME-LIFE LIBRARY OF BOATING
HUMAN BEHAVIOR
THE ART OF SEWING
THE OLD WEST
THE EMERGENCE OF MAN
THE AMERICAN WILDERNESS
THE TIME-LIFE ENCYCLOPEDIA OF GARDENING
LIFE LIBRARY OF PHOTOGRAPHY
THIS FABULOUS CENTURY
FOODS OF THE WORLD
TIME-LIFE LIBRARY OF AMERICA
TIME-LIFE LIBRARY OF ART
GREAT AGES OF MAN
LIFE SCIENCE LIBRARY
THE LIFE HISTORY OF THE UNITED STATES
TIME READING PROGRAM
LIFE NATURE LIBRARY
LIFE WORLD LIBRARY
FAMILY LIBRARY:
  HOW THINGS WORK IN YOUR HOME
  THE TIME-LIFE BOOK OF THE FAMILY CAR
  THE TIME-LIFE FAMILY LEGAL GUIDE
  THE TIME-LIFE BOOK OF FAMILY FINANCE

The Cover: During an engagement in 1645, the ship of Venetian commander Francesco Morosini leads two other high-sterned galleasses, supported by galleys *(left),* against Venice's longtime rival for supremacy in the eastern Mediterranean, the Ottoman Turks.

The Title Page: A cloud-dispelling burst of celestial light shines down its blessing upon the Venetian ship of state, shown plowing through rough seas of war in this allegorical silver coin minted in 1646. The Latin inscription on the edge boasts that Venice "shines among the waves."

THE VENETIANS

by Colin Thubron
AND THE EDITORS OF TIME-LIFE BOOKS

TIME-LIFE BOOKS, ALEXANDRIA, VIRGINIA

Time-Life Books Inc.
is a wholly owned subsidiary of

TIME INCORPORATED

FOUNDER: Henry R. Luce 1898-1967

Editor-in-Chief: Henry Anatole Grunwald
Chairman of the Board: Andrew Heiskell
President: James R. Shepley
Editorial Director: Ralph Graves
Vice Chairman: Arthur Temple

TIME-LIFE BOOKS INC.

MANAGING EDITOR: Jerry Korn
Executive Editor: David Maness
Assistant Managing Editors: Dale M. Brown (planning),
George Constable, George G. Daniels (acting),
Martin Mann, John Paul Porter
Art Director: Tom Suzuki
Chief of Research: David L. Harrison
Director of Photography: Robert G. Mason
Senior Text Editor: Diana Hirsh
Assistant Art Director: Arnold C. Holeywell
Assistant Chief of Research: Carolyn L. Sackett
Assistant Director of Photography: Dolores A. Littles

CHAIRMAN: Joan D. Manley
President: John D. McSweeney
Executive Vice Presidents: Carl G. Jaeger,
John Steven Maxwell, David J. Walsh
Vice Presidents: Nicholas Benton (public relations),
Nicholas J. C. Ingleton (Asia), James L. Mercer
(Europe/South Pacific), Herbert Sorkin (production),
Paul R. Stewart (marketing), Peter G. Barnes,
John L. Canova
Personnel Director: Beatrice T. Dobie
Consumer Affairs Director: Carol Flaumenhaft
Comptroller: George Artandi

The Seafarers

Editorial Staff for *The Venetians:*
Editor: Jim Hicks
Designer: Herbert H. Quarmby
Chief Researcher: W. Mark Hamilton
Text Editors: Anne Horan, Lydia Preston
Staff Writers: Gus Hedberg, Kumait N. Jawdat,
Teresa Pruden, David Thiemann
Researchers: Lois Gilman, Mindy A. Daniels,
Adrienne George, Philip Brandt George,
Frances R. Glennon, Ann Dusel Kuhns
Art Assistant: Michelle René Clay
Editorial Assistant: Ellen Prior Keir

Special Contributors
Jean I. Tennant (pictures); Sheldon Cotler (design);
Barbara Hicks (research)

Editorial Production
Production Editor: Douglas B. Graham
Operations Manager: Gennaro C. Esposito,
Gordon E. Buck (assistant)
Assistant Production Editor: Feliciano Madrid
Quality Control: Robert L. Young (director), James J. Cox
(assistant), Daniel J. McSweeney, Michael G. Wight
(associates)
Art Coordinator: Anne B. Landry
Copy Staff: Susan B. Galloway (chief), Anne T. Connell,
Sheirazada Hann, Celia Beattie
Picture Department: Betsy Donahue, Jane Martin

Correspondents: Elisabeth Kraemer (Bonn);
Margot Hapgood, Dorothy Bacon, Lesley Coleman
(London); Susan Jonas, Lucy T. Voulgaris (New York);
Maria Vincenza Aloisi, Josephine du Brusle (Paris);
Ann Natanson (Rome).
Valuable assistance was also provided by: Mehmet Ali
Kislali (Ankara); Martha Mader (Bonn); Mavis Airey,
Brigid Grauman (Brussels); Robert Kroon (Geneva); Judy
Aspinall (London); Jane Walker (Madrid); Carolyn T.
Chubet, Miriam Hsia, Christina Lieberman (New York);
Marie Thérèse Hirschkoff (Paris); Bianca Gabbrielli,
Mimi Murphy (Rome); Traudl Lessing (Vienna).

The Author:
Colin Thubron has written several books
about the Mediterranean world, including
Journey into Cyprus and, in the Time-Life
Books Great Cities series, *Jerusalem* and *Is-
tanbul.* A Fellow of the Royal Society of
Literature, he is also the author of the nov-
els *The God in the Mountain* and *Emperor.*
He boasts a formidable literary forebear:
He is descended from John Dryden, Eng-
land's first poet laureate.

The Consultants:
John Horace Parry is the Gardiner Professor of Oceanic History and Affairs at Harvard University. British born, he served as
a commander in the Royal Navy and is
a former President of the University of
Wales. His books include *Trade and Dominion* and *Europe and a Wider World*—
two volumes that are concerned with maritime exploration.

Frederic Chapin Lane is a former President of the American Historical Associ-
ation and is Professor Emeritus of History
at The Johns Hopkins University, where he
taught medieval and Renaissance history
for 35 years. Among his books are *Venetian Ships and Shipbuilders of the Renaissance* and *Venice: A Maritime Republic.*

Edward Muir, Assistant Professor of History at Syracuse University, is an authority
on state rituals in Venice during the Renaissance and has written numerous articles on Venetian history.

John Francis Guilmartin Jr. is a lieutenant
colonel in the United States Air Force and
a specialist in the history of arms. He is
editor of the *Air University Review* and the
author of *Gunpowder and Galleys: Chang-
ing Technology and Mediterranean Warfare at Sea in the 16th Century.*

For information about any Time-Life book, please write:
Reader Information, Time-Life Books,
541 North Fairbanks Court, Chicago, Illinois 60611.

TIME-LIFE is a trademark of Time Incorporated U.S.A.

Library of Congress Cataloguing in Publication Data
Thubron, Colin, 1939-
  The Venetians.
  (The Seafarers)
  Bibliography: p.
  Includes index.
  1. Venice—History—697-1508. 2. Venice—
History—Turkish Wars, 1453-1571. 3. Venice—
History—Turkish Wars, 17th century. 4. Crusades.
I. Time-Life Books. II. Title. III. Series: Seafarers.
DG677.5.T48   945'.31   80-136
ISBN 0-8094-2683-8
ISBN 0-8094-2682-X lib. bdg.

Contents

Chapter 1
An enduring union with the sea

Gondolas and galleys crowd alongside a quay in Venice in the 15th Century, when the republic was the center of Mediterranean trade.

eyond the long, sheltering isles of the Venetian lagoon, the sea was littered with ships. A faint sound of music, mingled with salvos of cannon and the pealing of church bells, swelled softly across the water, and crowds of men and women, leaning over the sides of their tapestry-draped boats, filled the air with song. Under the spring sun, the massed armor of soldiers gleamed in galleys and brigantines. And hosts of smaller craft—black gondolas of the citizenry, guild barges hung with bunting, and pilot boats filled with young noblemen—thronged like moths around the giant *Bucentaur*, a great golden flame of a ship 100 feet in length, whose long oars pushed her solemnly out to sea.

This was the state galley of the republic of Venice in the middle of the 15th Century, when the city reigned as the prime sea power of its age. Along the sides of the great ship, sculpted sea creatures frolicked and tumbled in abandon; high above the *Bucentaur's* red canopy billowed a huge banner that displayed the image of a winged lion, symbol of Saint Mark, the republic's patron saint; and at the prow a carved female figure representing Justice, with sword and scales in hand, gazed steadily out to sea.

Some 40 oars rose and fell in rhythm, carrying the *Bucentaur* through the waves like a fantastic marine centipede. Then, on the open sea, the rowing stopped. In the stern the Doge—chief dignitary of the republic—stepped forward from the throne, where he sat among state notables and his servants.

Sonorously he addressed the ocean: "We espouse thee, O Sea, in token of our true and perpetual dominion over thee." Then he took a gold wedding ring from his finger and cast it into the waters.

This ceremonial partnership with the sea had its origins back in the year 1000, when the republic crushed the pirates of Dalmatia, a region on the eastern shore of the Adriatic, with an expedition that was launched on Ascension Day. Every year thereafter, on Ascension Day, the city's bishop would solemnly bless the sea in a ceremony that was not only a thanksgiving for victory but a magic rite of propitiation: a ritual calming of the unpredictable deep. In the early 13th Century, after Venice had become a maritime empire, the strange and distinctive Marriage of the Sea was grafted onto the old blessing—a statement of imperial dominion and ownership, as of a husband over his wife's possessions. It was the high point of the Venetian year. Without this renewed pledge, some thought, the wealth-giving sea, like a jilted bride, would desert the city, taking her dowry with her.

Indeed the greatness, the very existence of Venice, was bound up with the sea. The city's empire was a sea empire: a scattering of harbors and islands along vital maritime ways. Its prosperity was based on twin enterprises: naval war and marine commerce. And these, in turn, depended, for much of its history, on two very different types of ship—the war galley (or longship) and the merchantman (the round ship).

Low and sleek, the war galley was propelled by both sail and oars and could outmaneuver the more cumbersome round ship. These swift galleys were built by state-employed craftsmen in the huge, crenelated bastion spreading east of the city—the Arsenal, a vast expanse of build-

Seated at the stern of the Bucentaur— the Venetian state vessel—the red-hatted Doge is rowed out to sea on Ascension Day to ritualistically wed the republic to the Adriatic. At the prow, behind a wooden figure of Justice, stand dignitaries bearing symbols of the authority of the Doge: an umbrella, trumpets, throne and eight furled banners. Another official stands on the canopy and serves as pilot for the ceremonial voyage.

ings and docks that by the 15th Century had become the greatest industrial complex in Europe.

The round ship, on the other hand, was constructed in Venice's flourishing private shipyards and went only by sail. Its beam was a third as great as its length, and it typically weighed up to 600 tons. In these broad-bellied merchantmen, the Venetians ventured into the Mediterranean, the Black Sea and even the Atlantic, carrying wines from Crete; sugar, cotton and grain from Egypt; and silver, copper and woolen cloth from as far away as Flanders and Britain.

In the late 13th Century the two ships were wedded into an extraordinary hybrid, the great galley, shaped like the war galley but wider and deeper. These awesome vessels, designed as merchantmen but later used also as warships, were built in the Arsenal and operated by the state. In them the Venetians garnered the luxury traffic of the East: the spices and drugs of the Indies brought by Arab and Indian merchants to the Red Sea, the silks of China, the gold thread and jewels of Byzantium.

For three centuries, between 1200 and 1500, Venice dominated the eastern Mediterranean, and for centuries before and afterward its strength was enormous. So long a history, of course, offers a dazzling complexity of enterprise. But in the republic's extraordinary saga of seafaring, there stand out two ferocious theaters of war—those of the crusaders and of the Ottoman Turks—and two remarkable fields of activity: the shipbuilding of the state Arsenal and the traffic with the Orient. Dangerous, but huge with promise, these challenges, fully met, turned Venice into the most glamorous city of its age.

The beginnings of this most remarkable of metropolises was attended by desperation and squalor. Early in the Fifth Century, when barbarian Goths and Huns fell on the rich pasturelands of northeast Italy, the frightened inhabitants began looking to the sea. Retreating to the watery maze of swamps fringing the northern Adriatic, they eked out a life as fishermen and traders in salt, shoring up their island refuges against the sea with walls of twisted willow boughs. Around them the once-mighty Roman Empire disintegrated, controlled in the West by barbarian tribes, dwindling in the East to a Byzantine state ruled from Constantinople.

The earliest account of their life comes from a time when Italy had fallen under the rule of a Germanic King, Theodoric the Ostrogoth. His prefect, Cassiodorus, wrote in 523 to ask the lagoon dwellers to ship wine and oil to the fortress at Ravenna, on Italy's northeastern coast. "For you live like sea birds," he wrote, "with your homes dispersed, like the Cyclades, across the surface of the water. The solidity of the earth on which they rest is secured only by osier and wattle; yet you do not hesitate to oppose so frail a bulwark to the wildness of the sea. Among you there is no difference between rich and poor; your food is the same, your houses are all alike. Envy, which rules the rest of the world, is unknown to you. Be diligent, therefore, to repair your boats—which, like horses, you keep tied up at the doors of your dwellings—and make haste to depart."

This request, oddly poetic for such an official, was evidently designed to flatter. Yet it pinpoints both the frugality and the comparative democracy of these marshland communities—traits that were to characterize Venice for much of its future.

The invasion of Italy by Lombard tribesmen in 568 sent many more refugees into the lagoons, and over the decades the scattered island peoples coalesced. Nominally subjects of the Byzantine Empire, they maintained a precarious semi-independence. Invading armies, struggling for control of the Italian mainland, either failed to overcome the island dwellers or reined in their horses before the marshy barrier of the lagoon and turned aside.

By the 10th Century, Venetian merchants—ideally situated as middlemen between the European West and the rich Byzantine East—had begun trading throughout the Adriatic. Some Venetian vessels pushed into the eastern Mediterranean and bartered with Muslim states, to the fury of pious Christians. Venice's industries expanded from the gathering of salt and fish to more sophisticated and lucrative activities: shipbuilding, iron and glass manufacture, dyeing and jewelry making.

To protect its growing trade and guard against pirates, Venice devel-

Venice depended upon these two complementary ships for its mercantile and military ventures across the Mediterranean and beyond. The broad, high-sitting round ship (right) made a commodious if rather unwieldy merchant vessel. The oar-equipped longship or galley (shown below in a sketch attributed to Raphael) put its greater speed and maneuverability to best use in battle.

oped a powerful war fleet. The city became more an ally of the gradually weakening Byzantine Empire than a vassal. A series of skillfully negotiated commercial treaties with the European Holy Roman Emperors and the Emperors of Byzantium—supplemented by trade agreements with Muslim states in North Africa—added to the republic's influence.

By the end of the 11th Century, Venice had grown into a formidable city-state, ruled by a doge, or duke, who was elected for life but who, over the centuries, became answerable to other elected officials. Above all, his power was subject to that of the Great Council, a group of prominent men that elected members of all the other advisory, judiciary and legislative bodies, including the Senate, which fashioned policy in matters of commerce and war. The doge, who generally reached his post late in life, served an average of 11 or 12 years. He and other elected officials customarily were chosen from a group of no more than 1,600 patrician families, most of whom had one thing in common: Their wealth and political power derived from trade.

Before the 11th Century ended, Venice had swollen into a rich, cosmopolitan city, but it was not yet the dreamlike Gothic metropolis it was destined to become. Rather, the city sprawled in a labyrinth of boat-strewn canals lined by houses of timber and thatch, with dwindling orchards and meadows in between. Here and there showed churches and palaces in brick and stone, and already St. Mark's Basilica was thrusting its domes and pinnacles into the sky. But the world of Venice was still a simple one: Its people dressed in plain gowns; its squares were paved only with beaten earth; and those islands not joined with piles were linked only by precarious wooden bridges, over which the richer citizens rode gingerly on humble mules.

Crowded onto their islands, the Venetians produced no class of land-owning feudal lords. Without the resources of farmland, without forests or rivers or quarries, they viewed the sea as their true country. They remained a nation of boatmen, and their aristocracy was dominated by an elite of merchant princes who rode the shifting political and economic tides of their times as skillfully as their ships rode the waves.

On November 27, 1095, as the 32nd Doge, Vitale Falier, lay dying, Pope Urban II called upon Christendom to deliver the Holy Land from the Saracens, the waves of Arabs and Turks that had flowed over the Middle East since the Seventh Century. Their possession of the Holy Land was a reproach to Christian Europe. The Pope's appeal—momentous for the whole Mediterranean world and beyond—marked the beginning of the Crusades. The princes and peasants of Europe responded alike. They came from Normandy, Flanders, France, Spain, England and Denmark. The Normans of Sicily and southern Italy added redoubtable forces, and the maritime republics of Pisa and Genoa, scenting new trade, supported the venture with fleets.

Only Venice held aloof. Although the city could, on occasion, display as much religious enthusiasm as the rest of medieval Christendom, it rarely allowed sentiment to interfere with the more practical preoccupations of commerce. The Venetians did not want to disrupt their profitable trade with Islam, nor did they wish to jeopardize their relationship with Constantinople by allying themselves with the European forces whose invasion of the Holy Land posed a potential threat to the power of the Byzantine Empire.

But in 1099 the crusaders captured Jerusalem. They massacred almost all of the Muslim inhabitants, burned most of the city's Jews alive in the chief synagogue and set up Godfrey of Bouillon, Duke of Lower Lorraine, as ruler. Although much of the region was still in Muslim hands and the fighting continued, the crusaders had achieved their main objective. They established a cluster of Christian principalities along the coasts of Syria and Palestine, creating a new balance of power in the East. Venice could no longer afford to neglect this. Genoa and Pisa—the city's bitterest commercial rivals—were already reaping profits from their involvement in the holy wars and were extending their trade routes into waters Venice had monopolized. When Godfrey appealed to the Venetians for provisions and for naval aid to bolster his occupying armies, the republic mustered 80 galleys and some 100 other craft. In the autumn of 1099 the Doge's son, Giovanni Michiel, with Venice's spiritual leader, the Bishop of Castello, at his side, raised the banner of the Cross and the standard of Saint Mark and sailed the great fleet, crammed with armed men, out into the Adriatic.

Nosing its way down the island-scattered Dalmatian coast, where it took on more men and provisions, the fleet turned the southern shores of Greece and arrived at Rhodes, hoping to winter quietly there. But by then the whole Mediterranean was in turmoil. While the Venetian ships were riding at anchor off Rhodes, a Pisan fleet appeared on the horizon in a belligerent mood. The Venetian leader Michiel, bemused by the Pisans' warlike formation, sent a boat under a flag of truce to remonstrate. But the Pisans, it seems, refused to talk.

Exactly what followed is lost in the vagueness and contradictions of history. The Pisans apparently had hesitated on realizing the size of the Venetian fleet. But it was too late. A part of the Venetian line fell on them and engaged them in a bloody struggle. The galleys locked together and their crews fought hand to hand. Twenty ships and 4,000 prisoners fell to the Venetians, who extorted from their rivals a promise (soon broken) to quit the eastern Mediterranean forever.

This engagement was an ugly portent, for it heralded a long, unhappy conflict among the maritime republics of Italy: Venice, Genoa, Pisa and Amalfi. Interspersed with armed and watchful truces, their wars continued for 300 years.

After the battle with the Pisans, the Venetians again delayed their progress toward the Holy Land by engaging in a piece of pious theft. On the nearby mainland of Asia Minor lay the ruins of Myra, bishopric of Saint Nicholas, the patron saint of sailors, who had been buried there in a handsome church. They decided to collect the saint's corpse and take it home as a holy relic. But when they reached Myra and broke open the cypress coffins in the great church, they discovered only the bodies of Saint Theodore and Saint Nicholas' uncle. The coffin of Saint Nicholas himself was empty. The Bishop of Castello, undismayed, fell on his knees and prayed for guidance. At once—so the story goes—a sweet fragrance emanated from beneath an obscure altar of the church. There,

Standing in the pulpit of the cathedral in Clermont, France, in November 1095, Pope Urban II calls on the assembled clergy to support his plan to rescue the Holy Land from the Turks. The Pope hoped the Crusade, by linking Europe's noblemen to a common cause, would halt their habitual quarreling.

still holding a fresh palm leaf from Jerusalem, lay the uncorrupted body of the saint. Jubilantly the soldiers embarked all three corpses and set sail at last for the Holy Land.

They arrived in June 1100 to find the crusader leader, Godfrey of Bouillon, dying of typhoid. When the fleet docked at Jaffa, he hurried down from Galilee to greet it, but collapsed in the hostel that he himself had built in the port. The following day he rallied a little and weakly received Michiel and the Bishop of Castello, who presented him with gifts of gold and silver vases.

Godfrey was desperate for naval aid to help capture enemy ports along the coast, and the Venetians drove a hard bargain. They demanded free trading rights throughout crusader lands; a church and a business quarter in every town; a third of any city that they helped to seize; and the entire city of Tripoli on the coast of Lebanon, one of the key seaports in the eastern Mediterranean. In return, the Venetians offered no more than a promise to remain in the Holy Land until August 15. By the time the negotiations were concluded it was already July.

At once plans were drawn up for a joint attack on the fortified Saracen ports of Acre and Haifa. Godfrey was too ill to fight, but his troops—and those of his bellicose Norman ally, Tancred—marched down from Jerusalem to the coast. While the army made its way north along the shore to Acre, the Venetians tried to sail alongside; but a strong north wind held them back. In the meantime, on July 18, Godfrey had died in Jerusalem.

His death threw the crusaders into disarray. But their leaders refused to give up the entire campaign when Venetian aid had been so dearly bought. Abandoning their plan to attack both ports, they decided to launch an assault only on Haifa, which was smaller than Acre and less heavily fortified. Within a few days the crusaders were camped on the heights of Mount Carmel above the town, awaiting the arrival of the Venetians. In the beleaguered city a small Egyptian garrison had distributed arms to the alarmed populace. The inhabitants of Haifa were mostly Jews, who remembered too well the fate of their people when the crusaders had captured Jerusalem the year before.

Meanwhile, the north wind dropped, and the Venetian squadron came sailing into the bay. There began a furious attack by sea and land. Seven Venetian siege catapults called mangonels pounded the walls with stones, while the soldiers wheeled a Venetian siege engine—a giant mobile fortress, wood-planked, and hung with protective hides—against the chief tower of the city. From within the device men began hacking at the tower's wall. Down on the ground heavy-mailed knights threw scaling ladders against the ramparts. But the Egyptians and Jews, knowing that they must hold out or be annihilated, defended their city with such desperate skill that the attackers became discouraged. At the same time Tancred discovered that Godfrey of Bouillon, shortly before his death, had promised that when Haifa fell it should be ceded to another nobleman. He retired to his tent in fury. The Venetians, after one of their galleys had been sunk before the sea walls, withdrew disheartened to the open sea. For almost a week the assault faltered. Then, with the time for the Venetian departure drawing close, Tancred and the knights roused themselves and attacked again.

In paired niches on a wall of Rheims Cathedral, a priest administers Communion to a crusader. Pope Urban II promised forgiveness of sins to all those who took the vow to free Jerusalem —and he threatened to excommunicate any man who did not keep the vow.

Their main hope of mounting the walls still lay in the enormous Venetian siege engine, which had been left stranded just outside the city's walls after the first attack had failed. Two French knights and a German knight now climbed up inside it. There, to their astonishment, they found a young Venetian who had refused to retreat with his compatriots. He cried out to the three men with joy and relief: "Let us stay united, in God's name, however few we are." The three knights, steeled by his words, were soon joined by 20 of Tancred's Normans, and together the little band vowed to take the main enemy tower or die in the attempt.

The attackers rolled the siege engine against the wall under a rain of flaming oil and pitch. From its partial shelter they attacked the tower with iron mattocks and double-bladed axes, while the Jews and Egyptians above tried to engulf them—men and machine together—in flames. All day and all night the struggle continued. By morning, if the 12th Century chronicler Albert of Aix is to be believed, the crusaders' shields were burned and lacerated to shreds in their mailed hands. Some of the knights had suffocated; others had been struck dead by the arrows and sling stones of the defenders. But on the morning of July 25 the garrison lost heart. The knights carried the tower by assault and opened the gates to the whole army, while the Venetian fleet came storming into the bay once more. A few of the city's defenders managed to escape. The rest were massacred.

Not long afterward, heavy with secular plunder and the dubious bones of their saints, the Venetian fleet weighed anchor and sailed for home. They timed their arrival for Saint Nicholas' day, and the whole of the city's populace was out to greet them. Reverently the presumed body of the saint was interred in the church of Saint Nicholas on the island of the Lido. No one knew—or admitted to knowing—that another corpse said to be that of Saint Nicholas had been stolen from its coffin in Myra 13 years earlier by merchants from Bari in southern Italy, where it lies enshrined to this day in a huge church consecrated by Pope Urban.

For the next two decades, while Venetian merchants profited from their new trading concessions, Venetian military squadrons were occupied in the Adriatic. Although the republic sent a fleet to the Holy Land in 1110 to help capture the port of Sidon—they fended off an Egyptian flotilla and received property in Acre as a reward—the crusaders' main naval support came from other maritime states. But by the spring of 1123 the existence of the whole precarious crusader kingdom was threatened by a renewed display of Saracen might: The King of Jerusalem was taken prisoner by the Muslims; a powerful Egyptian fleet controlled the waters off Palestine; and the Muslims held two key Palestinian ports, Ascalon and Tyre. Venice responded to a plea for aid by dispatching to the Holy Land a fleet of 72 men-of-war under the command of Doge Domenico Michiel, son of the leader of the 1099 expedition. Michiel dropped anchor off Acre in late May and heard that the Egyptian fleet was lying off Ascalon to the south.

Boldly the Venetians sought it out. From the bulk of his fleet Michiel selected 28 big war galleys, each propelled by 100 oars and 200 armed rowers, together with four larger vessels carrying baggage and siege weapons. He sent these four, whose size gave them the appearance of

In a 16th Century commemoration of an early Venetian victory over the rival maritime city-state of Pisa, the sword-wielding Venetian commander, Giovanni Michiel (left), urges his forces against the enemy as the two fleets clash off Rhodes in 1099.

merchantmen, several miles in front, as if they were alone. The mass of the warships followed, just below the horizon.

They approached the Egyptians at dawn. The sea was very calm, and the wind was behind them. The faint early light showed the Muslims what they thought to be an easy prey. Snatching up their oars, they rushed to the attack. But what they saw as the light hardened must have filled them with terror, for they suddenly realized that their quarry was not merchantmen but formidable warships. And close behind, running with the wind, a whole armada of galleys was bearing down on them.

The Venetian flagship, carrying the Doge himself, was the first to close on the enemy. She rammed the Egyptian commander's galley, all but capsizing that ship. The Muslim formation was thrown into confusion. The Venetians, picking their targets, rammed them with merciless accuracy, rowing so hard that they overturned many Egyptian galleys. They swarmed aboard other galleys, and bitter hand-to-hand fighting followed. The slaughter was terrible. A contemporary chronicler, William of Tyre, later wrote that many of the Venetians were covered from head to foot with the blood of the slain and that, for a circuit of two miles around, the sea was strewn with corpses.

Only a small remnant of the enemy's fleet escaped. And the Venetians went on to capture 10 Egyptian merchantmen that were laden with spices and silks. On the nearby coast the putrefaction of hundreds of washed-up bodies caused widespread plague, and for years afterward Christian mariners believed that the waters where the battle had been fought were too polluted to be crossed safely.

The Venetians' victory was greater than they knew. The Egyptian shipyards at Alexandria, ever short of good timber, never replaced the losses, and Egypt was effectively eliminated as a sea power in the Mediterranean for the next two centuries.

The Venetian fleet remained in the Holy Land for another 14 months to help the crusaders starve into subjection the redoubtable port of Tyre, the last Muslim stronghold on the coast. Typically, the Venetians first demanded from their allies a series of sweeping commercial concessions. Negotiations dragged on for months, but in the end the Venetians were promised a third of the property in Tyre and Ascalon, additional commercial quarters in other crusader-held towns, exemption from the usual tolls and customs duties, the freedom to use their own weights and measures in all transactions—a monumental concession to such sharp traders—and part of the annual revenue of Acre. Tyre fell in July 1124. The hostage King of Jerusalem was released by the Muslims the following month. By then the Venetians had sailed for home, having won for the crusaders undisputed control of the eastern Mediterranean.

But during the next two decades the Muslims struck back at the crusader dominions and gradually recovered much of the territory they had lost during the earlier years. Although Christian Europe launched two more major Crusades, the Second in 1145 and the Third in 1188, the knights were able to maintain only a precarious hold on their dwindling kingdom. By the end of the 12th Century they had lost even Jerusalem.

Venice's contribution to the Christian cause during the Second and Third Crusades consisted of little more than the profitable business of ferrying Christian pilgrims to crusader-held shrines and occasionally transporting soldiers and equipment. The republic's greatest crusading adventure—the one that would lift it to the status of an empire—came in the Fourth Crusade, nearly a century after the Battle of Ascalon, Venice's last previous major engagement on behalf of the Christians. This new drama played itself out not in the Holy Land, but at the heart of the Byzantine dominions—Constantinople.

Ever since 330 A.D., when Constantine the Great moved the government of the Roman Empire to Byzantium—renaming the new capital after himself—Constantinople had been a city of immense power and prestige. The barbarians who conquered the Western Roman Empire in the Fifth Century did not overrun the rich Eastern remnant, which lived on, as the Empire of Byzantium, for another 10 centuries. But during that time much of the Byzantine Empire was gnawed away by other invaders. In the Seventh Century, Arabs captured its southern provinces—Syria, Palestine, Egypt and North Africa. Four hundred years later the Seljuk Turks of Central Asia devoured the eastern half of its provinces in Asia Minor, and Norman seafarers seized its last foothold in southern Italy.

By the 13th Century, reduced to little more than Greece and western Asia Minor, the Empire was sick at heart. Travelers to Constantinople reported that the people lived like princes but were hopelessly effeminate. Byzantium's military organization had been eroded, and the theocratic emperors, with their cruel, decadent court, could not revitalize it. Yet the city and its shriveled territories lived on. An exotic mélange of Greek and Oriental, of classical culture and Christian mysticism, it was the most sophisticated power in the Mediterranean world. It was also, to its peril, enormously rich and a city of magical allure to the uncouth imagination of the West.

The relationship between Venice and Constantinople had always been a complex one. As the Empire weakened, it began to rely on Venetian fleets to protect its western waters, and in return Venice was granted generous trading privileges. During the 12th Century the two powers became direct rivals for the trade of the eastern Mediterranean. The many Venetians who had established themselves in Byzantium during the years when the two powers were firm allies were hated for their arrogance and envied for their success. In 1118 the Byzantines temporarily withdrew all of Venice's commercial privileges in their Empire and negotiated treaties with the rival republic of Pisa. Venice and Byzantium reunited briefly in 1148 to fight the Norman rulers of southern Italy, whose attacks on Greece were undermining the interests of both. But the wounds had not healed. While the joint Byzantine and Venetian fleet was anchored off Corfu, some Venetian seamen, in full view of their allies, dressed up a colossal Ethiopian slave in Byzantine imperial vestments and staged a mock coronation on the poop of a captured galley. The Emperor never forgave them.

In 1171 all the Venetians in the Byzantine Empire were arrested and their property impounded. The republic retaliated with a naval expedition, but it was decimated by plague. Although the Byzantine measures against them were rescinded soon afterward, the Venetians did not forget. Indeed, the eyes of the whole West were focusing more sharply now on Constantinople. Europe not only envied Byzantium its wealth but was prejudiced against it for a religious reason: the traditional antipathy between Eastern Orthodox Christianity and Western Latin Christianity. This alienation deepened when the Byzantines offered only lukewarm support against Islam during the first three Crusades; they were considered not only heretics but traitors.

The West's opportunity to establish dominance over Constantinople and Venice's chance for revenge came with an upsurge of crusading sentiment in 1199, soon after the accession of Pope Innocent III. The new Pope called on Christendom once more to deliver Jerusalem from the Saracens. The powerful nobles of northern France and Flanders—Counts Louis of Blois, Theobald of Champagne and Baldwin of Flanders—responded by laying plans for a mighty expedition to the Holy Land. They estimated that their forces would number more than 30,000. Where could transport be found for such an army but in Venice?

In the spring of 1201 a party of six crusader envoys, led by Geoffrey of Villehardouin, Marshal of Champagne, arrived in the city to negotiate terms. Villehardouin, who left a graphic and statesman-like record of the whole Crusade, tells how Doge Enrico Dandolo agreed to transport an army of 4,500 knights and their horses, 9,000 squires and 20,000 foot soldiers; feed it for a year; and support it with 50 armed galleys. In exchange for their aid, the Venetians were to receive 85,000 silver marks—twice the annual revenue of the King of France—and half of the Crusade's joint conquests. But first the Doge had to gain the consent of the people. After the agreement had been drawn up, some 10,000 Venetians assembled around St. Mark's Basilica, where Villehardouin himself, in an emotional appeal, declared that he and his companions would kneel and not rise until they had won support for their expedition to the beleaguered Holy Land.

"Thereupon the six envoys," Villehardouin related, "in floods of tears, knelt at the feet of the assembled people. The Doge and all the other Venetians present also burst out weeping, and holding up their hands toward heaven, cried out with one accord: 'We consent! We consent!' There was such an uproar and such a tumult that you might have thought the whole world was crumbling to pieces."

Yet from then on the plans went awry. Theobald of Champagne, the expedition's popular young leader, died, and preparations faltered until the crusaders chose a successor, the powerful Italian noble, Boniface of Montferrat. Then the secret leaked out that the crusader leaders' real destination was not the Holy Land but Egypt, which they considered the weak point of the Muslim dominions. To the largely pious rank and file of the soldiers, Jerusalem, site of the Holy Sepulcher, could be the only worthy destination. Some of them defected; others made their way to Palestine by lesser ports. When the main forces began straggling into Venice in the summer of 1202, they numbered only a third of those promised. The deeply embarrassed nobles were unable to raise the money to pay for the Venetian squadron that had been built to transport an army three times their number. Even after the barons had given much of their private money, the sum fell short of the promised total by 34,000

With shining eyes that belie his blindness, the aged Doge Enrico Dandolo gazes forth from this 19th Century engraving with the intensity and firmness of purpose that made him a marvel to his age. The shrewd old patriot served the Venetian republic well into his eighties, having been a soldier and the Ambassador to the Byzantine court before being elected Doge in January 1193.

marks. The Venetians, who had suspended their own trade for more than a year in order to prepare for the expedition—and who had constructed a massive fleet of galleys, troop ships and horse transports suited only for a military operation—stood to lose a fortune. The whole Crusade was on the brink of disintegration.

Everything now rested with the Doge, Enrico Dandolo. He was an extraordinary man. Subtle, indomitable and a fanatical patriot, he was already about 85 years old, perhaps older, and was nearly stone-blind. One account has it that, while on a peace mission to the Byzantines in 1172, the vain and stubborn Dandolo so annoyed Emperor Manuel that the ruler had him partially blinded—a common Byzantine punishment. But more likely Villehardouin was right when he said that "although his eyes appeared bright and clear" Dandolo had "lost his sight through a wound in the head."

Whatever the cause of his affliction, neither age nor sightlessness seems to have blunted the Doge's mind or spirit. He quickly proposed to the crusaders that they postpone further payments until plunder should make good the debt. But in exchange for this concession they must recapture for Venice the powerfully fortified Dalmatian town of Zara, which 16 years earlier had defected to the King of Hungary, a Christian monarch desirous of an outlet in the Mediterranean.

The crusaders had no choice but to agree. Dandolo was threatening to cut off supplies to their army, which was stranded on the Lido, the long, narrow island across the mouth of the Venetian lagoon. The official papal representative to the Crusade, knowing that the Pope would be furious when he heard of the plans to attack a Christian power, tried to stop the assault on Zara. But Dandolo, refusing to acknowledge the legate's authority, bluntly told him that if he wished to minister to the army he could sail with it. If not, he could go back to Rome.

On September 8, Dandolo staged another ceremony at St. Mark's Basilica. Mounting the pulpit before the assembled notables, he declared, "I am an old man, weak and in need of rest, and my health is failing." But then, to the astonishment of all, he announced that he himself would lead the Venetians in the Crusade, and he knelt at the altar in tears while a cross was sewed onto the front of his great cotton cap. Caught up in the emotion of the moment, many Venetians—most of whom had planned to stay home—took the vow of the Cross with him.

In the first week of October 1202, some three months later than intended, the Fourth Crusade sailed out of the Venetian lagoon. The fleet, numbering more than 200 ships, was the largest ever seen in those waters. At its head, in a vermilion-painted galley, went Dandolo, shaded by a silken awning, with the huge gold-and-crimson banner of Saint Mark unfurled above him. Cymbals clashed and four trumpeters blew their silver trumpets from the bow. On the poops of the warships, priests intoned the *Veni creator spiritus*—"Come, Holy Ghost, our souls inspire"—and from the fortified bows and sterns, hung with the shields of the knights and streaming with their pennants, the roars and shouts of the soldiery, the thudding of drums and the blaring of 200 trumpets all sounded together as though the Last Judgment were at hand. Each crusader leader commanded his own flotilla, and three huge transports in

Bearing flags emblazoned with the Lion of Saint Mark—the proud symbol of Venice—crusaders scale the walls of the Adriatic port of Zara while some of their comrades try to batter through a city gate. Anachronistic Renaissance costumes betray the fact that this scene was painted in the late 1500s, more than three centuries after the Venetians leveled the Dalmatian city in the hope of ridding the Adriatic of Zara's pirates.

particular stood out: the *Paradise,* the *Eagle* and the *Pilgrim.* Sailing with these massive vessels were wide-bowed landing craft and giant galleys bristling with more than 300 stone-throwing mangonels and even more powerful catapults called petraries.

As the crusaders reached open waters and spread their sails, wrote the knight Robert of Clari, "it seemed indeed as if the sea were all a-tremble and all on fire with the ships they were sailing and the great joy they were making."

On November 10, after stopping several times en route to take on supplies, the fleet arrived off Zara. In the bright, clear morning the galleys assembled, charged the chain that was stretched across the entrance of the city's harbor, and broke it. For two weeks the battle raged. From land, mangonels and petraries bombarded the city towers. From the sea, the troops attacked the walls with scaling ladders set up on the ships.

When Zara's defenders saw that the enemy was undermining their fortifications, they surrendered. The Doge occupied the city for the republic and divided the spoils equally between the crusaders and the Venetians. (Nonetheless, ferocious disputes broke out between the conquerors three days later.) Meanwhile, knowing that they had incurred papal wrath by attacking Zara, the crusaders sent emissaries to Rome to beg forgiveness. Pope Innocent granted the supplicant crusaders absolution but angrily excommunicated the unrepentant Venetians. Boniface of Montferrat, fearing that news of the Pope's action would cause turmoil in the ranks, kept it a secret. Thus the edict had no practical effect. As the Crusade continued, the Pope's fury subsided, and he made no attempt to enforce his decree.

Constantinople entered the crusaders' plans while the fleet and army were wintering in Zara. Envoys from a young Byzantine prince named Alexius arrived in Zara carrying a series of tempting proposals. The Prince, in fact, was an exile, with no fortune but his title. His father, Emperor Isaac II Angelus, languished in prison in Constantinople, blinded by his own brother, who had usurped the throne. Young Alexius promised to pay the crusaders the immense sum of 200,000 silver marks, to be divided equally between them and the Venetians, if they would restore him and his father to the purple. In addition he offered to provision the army for a year, to maintain 500 knights who would serve in the Holy Land, and personally to lead 10,000 Byzantine soldiers on the Crusade against Egypt. Finally, he would bring the Orthodox Church into communion with Rome.

A number of the more pious or disillusioned crusaders objected to attacking yet another Christian power when they had enlisted to fight Muslims. When Alexius' proposals were accepted by their leaders, some deserted the army overland and were massacred by the local inhabitants; others took to the sea, where many vanished in storms. But the great majority acceded to the idea, a few cynically, most of them piously. Many believed that the conquest of Byzantium was a practical step on the way to subjugating Muslim Egypt, and almost all were motivated by the long-standing hatred of the Latin West for the heretical East.

In April 1203 Alexius landed at Zara, and within a few days the fleet sailed for Constantinople. Slowly the ships circled Peloponnesian

Greece and entered the Aegean Sea. They penetrated the Dardanelles without resistance and at last sailed over the Sea of Marmara toward the great capital of the East.

Within the city, it seems, there prevailed at first a strange lassitude. The approach of the crusaders took the people by surprise; they were unsure of the fleet's purpose. The usurping Emperor, Alexius III, was a dissolute voluptuary. Ever since he had imprisoned and blinded his brother, he had been prey to morbid guilt and a fear of retribution. He offered his subjects little in the way of leadership.

The Byzantine imperial army, although 60,000 strong, was lightly armed and undisciplined. Its backbone, in fact, consisted of mercenaries drawn from all over Europe. Of these, a large Frankish contingent was suspected of sympathizing with the crusaders' cause; the Slavs and the Petchenegs from southwest Russia were restless and grasping. Only the elite Varangian Guard—mustachioed Britons and Danes whose ancestors had made their way to Constantinople in the 10th and 11th Centuries—could be counted on for unswerving loyalty. The effete Byzantines had always regarded these ax-wielding warriors—whose name derived from an old Norse word meaning "fidelity"—with astonishment. "They have yellow or russet hair and blue eyes," wrote the Byzantine historian Leo the Deacon. "They never allow themselves to be taken in battle and will kill themselves rather than surrender."

The imperial fleet was in even worse condition than the army. Only 16 years earlier the Byzantines had paid the Venetians themselves to build and man galleys in the Empire's defense. But the Emperor had neglected to maintain his navy. According to Nicetas Choniates, a former Byzantine state secretary who later wrote an anguished chronicle of his city's decline, the Emperor had refused to fell timber for shipbuilding because he enjoyed hunting in the woods, and the imperial eunuchs guarded the forests with the fervor of the Angel of Death guarding Eden. The navy had suffered further under the stewardship of the corrupt Byzantine Lord Admiral, Michael Stryphnos, who had sold off much of the existing ships' equipment—sails, anchors, rigging and all—for his own gain. Now the imperial war fleet consisted of 20 worm-eaten vessels rotting in the city's inner harbor.

Yet the approaching crusaders faced a formidable city—the largest, richest and most populous in the Mediterranean world. "Those who had never seen Constantinople before," wrote Villehardouin, "gazed very intently at the city, having never imagined there could be so fine a place in all the world. They noted the high walls and lofty towers encircling it and its rich palaces and tall churches, of which there were so many that no one would have believed it to be true if he had not seen it with his own eyes, and viewed the length and breadth of the city that reigns supreme over all others. There was indeed no man so brave and daring that his flesh did not shudder at the sight."

They may well have despaired, for Constantinople was the most magnificently fortified metropolis in the world, and it had never been successfully stormed. It lay on a triangular peninsula on the European shore of the Bosporus, lapped on one side by the Sea of Marmara and on the other by the sheltered inlet of the Golden Horn (page 31). Along these

Prince Alexius of Byzantium bends his knee to a gracious Doge Enrico Dandolo to ask the help of the crusaders in winning back the throne that had been usurped by his uncle. Despite his childlike appearance in this romanticized portrayal, Alexius was probably about 20 years old when he sought out the forces of Western Christendom at Zara in 1203.

shores a curtain of giant sea walls, studded with some 300 towers, jutted up from the sea. Across the Golden Horn, protecting the imperial ships, was slung a 500-yard chain, every link as long as a man's forearm.

Yet these defenses were puny compared with those on the landward side. There, across the three-mile neck of the peninsula, the Fifth Century Emperor Theodosius II had erected a triple bulwark. First there was a wide moat and breastwork, beyond which rose a 25-foot wall thickened by 96 towers spaced 100 yards apart. Finally, looming out of a 40-foot inner wall, were 96 square and polygonal bastions some 70 feet high. Over the centuries, invading armies—Persian, Slav and Saracen alike— had dashed themselves against these ramparts in vain. Even Attila the Hun, "the Scourge of God," had turned his hordes from the sight.

The crusaders, cruising under the sea walls on their arrival, did little but gape at the defenses, which left them, wrote Robert of Clari, "dumb with amazement." That night they retired to the far side of the Bosporus to forage. From the city the lights of their encampment could be seen in the darkness, scattered like a blaze of stars.

Any Byzantine hopes that the crusaders would go away were quickly disappointed. The fleetless Lord Admiral Stryphnos, reduced to scouting out the enemy with 500 cavalry, was ignominiously routed by 80 French knights. Soon afterward an imperial envoy sent to the crusader camp was dismissed with a message of defiance, and several heavily armed Venetian galleys patrolled under the city's ramparts, showing the young Prince Alexius to the people crowded on the walls and proclaiming him their rightful Emperor. The bemused citizens shouted back: "We have never heard of him!"

For the next three days the crusaders prepared their attack. Although the combined Venetian and crusader forces numbered some 20,000 men, they were keenly aware of the dangers that lay ahead. After their divisions were assembled, the clergy addressed the troops. Every man, wrote Villehardouin, made his confession and drew up his will.

Early on the morning of July 5 the crusaders boarded their ships and crossed the Bosporus, heading toward the northern shore of the Golden Horn. There Emperor Alexius III had drawn up a heavy force, which he led in person. The Venetian galleys moved in, with Doge Dandolo in the van. Then came the trained archers and crossbowmen of Baldwin, Count of Flanders, sweeping the shore with a fierce fire. In their wake were the ships of his brother Henri, then those of the Count of St. Pol, the powerful division of Count Louis of Blois, the knights of Champagne under Matthew of Montmorency, and the forces of Burgundy. Finally came the squadron of the commander, Boniface of Montferrat, carrying the Italian and German contingents.

For a moment it seemed as if the Byzantines would put up resistance. But the landing of the crusaders terrified them. They had never seen anything like it. Mailed and plated from head to foot like reptiles, the knights plunged waist-high into the sea, with their helmets laced, their lances in hand and their sergeants and bowmen behind them. Huge horse transports beached and opened their drawbridges, and the monstrous chargers, their quilted caparisons trailing through the water, were rushed to shore by the squires. Some knights, already mounted, charged straight off the lowered drawbridges. Their helmets—iron barrels with mere slits for eyes—invested them with a ghoulish inhumanity. No sooner had they couched their lances than the defenders fled, with Emperor Alexius in the lead.

This encounter was only the beginning. The crusaders next turned their attention to a massive tower that stood nearby, guarding the chain across the mouth of the Golden Horn. If the chain could be lowered or broken, the northern sea walls of Constantinople would be exposed to the Venetian fleet, and the ships in the harbor could be smashed.

The next morning the Byzantines ferried forces over to join the tower's garrison in a forlorn attempt to defend the outpost. But the crusaders outnumbered them. Within minutes the reinforcements were hurled back to their boats, and the garrison was fighting for its life at the base of the tower. By now the knights were pressing the defenders so hard that the tower's gateway, crowded with men, could not be closed. A stubborn, bloody fight raged around it. Meanwhile the Venetian ships eased forward to the harbor's mouth and repeatedly charged the great protective chain. Finally the mammoth *Eagle*, opening her sails to a strong wind, broke through the chain and burst into the harbor. Behind her the other ships closed in on the moribund Byzantine vessels, capturing or destroying all of them. There was little resistance.

With the tower taken and the harbor in their hands, the crusaders prepared to launch a direct assault on the northwest corner of the city, where the fortified imperial palace overlooked the waters of the Golden Horn. The Venetians, it was decided, would attack from the harbor and storm the sea walls with their galleys; the knights would fight by land.

On July 11, 1203, five days after the capture of the Horn, the crusader divisions crossed to the inlet's southern side and camped close to the city—so close, in one place, that the Byzantines could talk to them. There, the crusaders brought their mangonels to bear on the walls of the beautiful Blachernae Palace and slowly began to pulverize it.

But the Byzantines gave them no peace. They sallied out continuously from different gates, forcing the crusaders to enclose their camp with wooden palisades. The knights slept, ate and rested in full armor. "The whole camp," wrote Villehardouin, "had to be called to arms about six or seven times a day." Meanwhile, they were growing short of supplies. The only fresh meat was that of wounded horses, and in all there was only enough food for another three weeks.

The Venetians labored to transform their fleet into floating assault works. By removing the 100-foot yards of their large transports' lateen sails, laying pairs of those spars side by side and lashing planks across them, they created long, sturdy gangways—flying bridges. These, protected from arrows by wetted hides and canvas, were hoisted to the masts and anchored there with rope tackles. Rigged so that they could easily be raised or lowered, they hung out in front of the ships' poops like cranes, lifted at a slight angle, ready to alight on the city towers.

On July 17 the great assault was launched simultaneously by land and sea. The French wheeled mobile towers and battering rams against the walls and rushed up with scaling ladders at the first sign of a breach in the defenses. They were met by the long-haired Varangian Guard, and

Venetian transports, hung with crusaders' shields and laden
with mailed soldiers, ride at anchor off Constantinople in 1203
prior to the siege of the Byzantine capital. The painter of
this 15th Century French manuscript illumination erroneously
located Constantinople on a hill far from the water and made
the ships look like those of his own era; 13th Century Venetian
vessels were smaller and had side rather than stern rudders.

the terrible spiked axes of the Danes and Britons were pitted against the heavy French swords. Fifteen crusader knights and sergeants managed to gain a precarious foothold on the palace outwork, but the Varangians ferociously cut most of them down. At last the French withdrew, leaving behind many dead and two prisoners, who were led off to be displayed before Emperor Alexius.

The Venetian ships, meanwhile, surged across the Golden Horn in a massed formation some 1,200 yards wide. First came the transports, sending a shower of stones from the mangonels on their poops, to cover the landing. As the ships neared the walls, the men dangling far out on the flying bridges began exchanging blows in midair with the city's garrison. Then came the galleys all in line, filled with soldiers and bowmen, rowing swiftly with great sweeps of their oars.

But at this critical moment the Venetians momentarily lost their nerve. The galleys hung back just offshore, their overawed captains looking vainly for a weakness in the colossal sea walls. "And here was an extraordinary feat of boldness," wrote Villehardouin. "For the Doge of Venice, who was an old man and stone-blind, stood fully armed on the prow of his galley, with the banner of Saint Mark before him, and cried out to his men to drive the ship ashore if they valued their skins. And so they did and ran the galley ashore, and he and they leaped down and planted the banner before him in the ground. And when the other Venetians saw the standard of Saint Mark and the Doge's galley beached before their own, they were ashamed and followed him ashore."

The moment they beached, the men rushed their scaling ladders to the foot of the walls. Above them the bastions rose sheer. Huge rocks were tipped down on them, and they knew that Greek fire—an inflammable compound of sulfur, pitch, niter and oil, ejected from tubes—might at any moment explode in their faces or burn them alive in their armor. But the orders of the sightless octogenarian Doge flailed them on. The bolts from their crossbows filled the air with a metal tempest, and the transports, their gangways hovering over the enemy ramparts like predatory beaks, moved swiftly into the gaps left between the galleys. The gangways came crashing down on the towers, and the soldiers charged over the walls three abreast. Momentarily the banner of Saint Mark appeared on one of the towers, then vanished, its bearer slain. But the attack went on. The Venetians swarmed up the scaling ladders, lurched across the flying bridges and pounded the enemy with stones and arrows from every angle. They cleared a bloody path across the battlements and within an hour had captured 25 towers and opened the city gates. Jubilantly they collared Byzantine war horses and sent them around in boats to the hard-pressed crusader land force.

Emperor Alexius III desperately shunted reinforcements into the beleaguered section of the city. The advancing Venetians, with the wind to their backs, responded by setting fire to houses, sending a screen of smoke and flames beating toward the Byzantines and devastating a whole district of Constantinople.

To divert the Venetians, Alexius led all his immense but unreliable force—the "flower of the city's youth," wrote Choniates—against the crusader camp outside the walls. The knights were so outnumbered, wrote Robert of Clari, that they hurriedly armed their cooks and stable lads and "had them fitted out with quilts and saddlecloths and copper pots and maces and pestles, and they were so ugly and hideous that the common foot soldiers of the Emperor, who were in front of the walls, had great fear and terror when they saw them." The lightly armed masses of the Emperor's regiments and the iron wedge of the crusaders moved toward each other, each up gentle inclines. But as the men crested the top of the rise and saw one another, they stopped. Meanwhile, hearing of the threat to the crusader land troops, the Doge withdrew his men from the walls to go to the aid of his allies. Having achieved their object of relieving Venetian pressure on the city, the Byzantines gradually retreated and filtered away.

Thus, after a whole day's fighting, nothing had been gained. The Byzantines reoccupied their walls, and the Venetian ships pulled back across the harbor. The siege seemed to have reached a deadlock.

That night the pusillanimous Emperor Alexius III, deserting his people and his wife, Euphrosyne—but taking along his favorite daughter, Irene, and several concubines—gathered up 1,000 pounds of gold and a hoard of precious stones and secretly fled the city. The Byzantines woke to find themselves leaderless. At once they hauled the old and blinded Isaac II Angelus out of his prison and set him once more on the imperial throne. It was a clever move. Isaac Angelus was a weak, suspicious old man whose previous reign had been disastrous—he had sold government offices like vegetables, wrote Choniates—but he was the lawful ruler and the father of the young Alexius, the crusaders' protégé. His return cut the moral ground from under the young claimant's feet.

Villehardouin later described how he and a deputation of three others, including two Venetians, were let into the city that morning to present terms to the restored Emperor. When the envoys entered the throne room, they were dazed by the brilliance of the quasi-Oriental court. Over the preceding 900 years the Byzantines had evolved a hieratic, almost balletic ceremonial. To his subjects the Emperor was the high priest of God on earth, and his court a mystical foretaste of paradise. The women's glistening robes and pearl-encrusted diadems, the eunuchs' voluminous silks, the effete generals' elaborate armor all jostled and blazed together in a hall glowing with mosaics and polychrome marble. At the end sat the blind Emperor, dressed in purple, and pale from years of prison; his beautiful Empress, sister of the King of Hungary, sat at his side.

Villehardouin and the other envoys presented the crusaders' proposals to the old man in secret, in another room. The money that young Alexius had promised must be paid; the Byzantine soldiers that had been promised for the Holy Land must be sent; the Eastern Church must be placed within the jurisdiction of Rome; and Prince Alexius must be instated as co-Emperor with his father. The old man grudgingly assented to all of the demands.

On August 1 young Alexius IV was crowned beside his father. The crusaders, camped on the far side of the Golden Horn, awaited payment, killing the time by touring the city. But Alexius could not find the money. He emptied the imperial coffers and melted down church plate; but it was not enough. Local resentment toward the rapacious crusaders

As seen in this stylized 15th Century map, massive walls shielded Constantinople from attack by either land or sea. During the assault by the crusaders in 1203, Venetian ships sailed up the Bosporus— the strait that separated the peninsular capital (left) from the coast of Asia Minor (right)—then stormed the city walls from the Golden Horn, the inlet between Constantinople and its suburb of Pera.

PERA

pera

CONSTAN =
TINOPOLIS.

Porta delmelo

Sctus

Scti demet

Scti geor
ninus

Turquia

palaus Impatoris

chiramoa

rctus olim
palaij im
patoris

perra

Calchidona

Sctus Johes d
andre

Vlanga

Portus fed deftrua
precepto teucrorū

mounted daily. Within weeks rioting broke out, and some of the crusaders started a fire that raged for days, cutting a path three miles wide through the city's heart. Old Emperor Isaac could not keep pace with affairs. He devoted himself to his astrologers, who repeatedly assured him that he would prevail.

The key to the impasse lay with Venice and Dandolo. The crusading knights were anxious to leave for the Holy Land but were still deeply in debt to the Venetians. In November, according to Robert of Clari, the wily old Doge had himself rowed across the Horn in a galley while young Alexius IV came down on horseback to talk with him. "Alexius, what do you think you are doing?" demanded Dandolo. "Remember how we rescued you from utter misery and had you crowned Emperor. Will you not keep your trust with us and pay your debts?"

"No," replied the Emperor. "I will do no more than I have." And indeed he could not.

But the Doge was relentless. "No?" he called out. "Foolish boy, we hauled you up out of the dung! And we will throw you back into the dung again! I warn you that from now on I shall do all I can to bring about your downfall."

The break was complete. Soon afterward Alexius had 17 enormous merchant ships piled with logs, old wooden barrels and pitch. The vessels were set ablaze and sent with spread sails into the Golden Horn to burn the Venetian fleet. On two separate nights they bore down on the packed ships, filling the darkness with flames. But the Venetian mariners held the fire ships clear with grappling hooks, then towed them out into the mainstream of the Bosporus, where they were swept like fireflies out into the night.

Alexius had brought ruin on himself. He had alienated not only the crusaders, but his own people, who blamed him for their tribulations and branded him both a traitor and a heretic. The clergy, in particular, loathed him for plotting their subjugation to Rome. In January 1204, the nobleman Alexius Ducas, nicknamed Mourtzouphlus (a concocted term probably based on the old Greek words for "mad-browed," because of his shaggy eyebrows that joined in the middle), rushed into the young Emperor's apartment at night and told him that the palace was being attacked. Muffled in a long cloak, the unsuspecting Alexius was hurried out a side door, then treacherously cast into a dungeon, where 10 days later Mourtzouphlus had him strangled. Meanwhile, the ailing Isaac II Angelus, overcome by fear when he heard the news of his son's imprisonment, also died.

With the deaths of the two rulers, renewed war between the Byzantines and the crusaders was inevitable.

Mourtzouphlus, crowned Alexius V, possessed the energy that his predecessors had lacked. Over the next two months he repaired the sea walls and topped them with 40-foot wooden towers. Dandolo and the Venetians meanwhile mounted new catapults on the decks of their ships; encased the vessels in protective timber, vines and hides; and lengthened their flying bridges to match the enemy towers. But when they attacked on the morning of April 9 an unfavorable wind held most of the ships from the walls, and the Byzantine catapults, high on top of

In an 11th Century depiction of an amphibious siege, soldiers charge across flying bridges—makeshift gangways hung from ships' masts. The flying bridges used by Venetians in the assault on Constantinople were "so wide"—wrote crusader Robert of Clari—"that three knights in armor could go side by side."

the towers, reaped a terrible harvest in the fleet. On land, the crusaders' battering-rams and their crews were crushed by boulders pushed over the city's ramparts. By midafternoon the attackers were reembarking their men and retreating across the Horn. The Byzantines, wrote Robert of Clari, hooted and jeered from the battlements, "and let down their clouts and showed them their backsides."

But three days later the crusaders had returned, grimmer and harder than ever. In token of a new-found piety, they had even driven the prostitutes from their camp. The bishops had blessed the whole army and promised paradise to those who fell in combat. This time it was to be a trial to the death.

At midday on April 12 the fleet advanced en masse on a front more than two miles wide. The Venetians had lashed their largest ships together in pairs, enabling them to throw broad platforms filled with armed men against each tower. These floating bulwarks moved across the harbor in terrible unison, cushioned from the enemy's boulders by their makeshift timber palisades and bundles of grapevines.

Inside the city, on a gentle mound a little behind the walls, Emperor Mourtzouphlus had pitched a scarlet tent and was directing his men in person. The citizens were now so confident that "all along the walls and towers," wrote Villehardouin, "there was nothing to be seen but people. Then began a fierce and magnificent assault, as each ship steered a straight course forward." From the city's new towers some 60 catapults released a deluge of stones at the fleet. The crusaders' Greek fire exploded harmlessly against the hides that covered the wooden towers. The flying bridges, hovering clumsily from the mastheads, searched for openings. But in the entire fleet only four or five ships were tall enough to overtop the rebuilt walls.

What happened next seemed providential to the crusaders. As Villehardouin piously wrote, "Our Lord raised for us a north wind." It blew across the Horn, lifting the prows of the vessels over the mud flats under the walls and nudging them forward. The giant ships *Pilgrim* and *Paradise*, bound together, rammed against one of the towers. On the *Pilgrim's* flying bridge two French knights and an obscure Venetian named Pietro Alberti stood poised to attack. As the ship struck, Alberti grasped the sides of the tower window and levered himself inside. Behind him the ships, swaying at the mercy of the wind, drifted back and isolated him. "When he was inside," wrote Robert of Clari, "and the sergeants who were in this tower—Englishmen, Danes and Greeks—looked around and saw him, they rushed at him with axes and swords and cut him to pieces. And as the sea carried the ship forward to strike against the tower once again, one of the two knights, Andrew of Dureboise, took hold of the sides of the window with hands and feet and pulled himself inside on his knees. As he entered, they rushed on him with axes and swords and struck him fiercely, but, because of his armor, by God's mercy they did not wound him."

This intrepid knight, to the defenders' astonishment, got to his feet and attacked them. The whole tower was thrown into confusion. Soon the second knight joined him, followed by soldiers who lashed the *Pilgrim* to the tower, creating a powerful bridgehead. But when the sea ebbed the ship threatened to pull down the whole superstructure, and they were forced to loose the cables. Nearby, another tower was carried by assault from another flying bridge; but the battlements all around were so crowded with defending soldiers that the crusaders could not advance any further.

Then a French nobleman, Pierre of Amiens, stormed out of another ship with 60 sergeants and 10 knights (including Robert of Clari), and attacked a bricked-up postern, a small gate at the foot of the walls, gouging at it with picks and axes. An appalling rain of Greek fire burst on their raised shields, and boiling pitch and boulders splattered and crashed down on them. They finally prized a hole in the rampart but stared through at so many men that they were afraid to enter.

But Aleaumes of Clari, Robert of Clari's brother—a fighting priest, it seems—got on his hands and knees and started to crawl through the breach. Robert, horrified, grabbed him by the foot and tried to pull him back, and for a moment the two brothers tugged and jostled in undignified disunion. Finally, wrote Robert, Aleaumes escaped him and pro-

A sailor perched atop the mast of a high-sided Venetian horse transport (top) trumpets a call to battle in one scene from a series of 13th Century mosaics that chronicle events of the Fourth Crusade. In the vignette at the bottom, three vanquished Byzantine warriors vainly appeal to a crusader for clemency.

ceeded through the gap, slashing at his attackers and calling on the rest to follow him. Within minutes all 70 men were inside the walls and were breaking down the nearest gate.

Soon two more gates were driven open while the closest galleys and transport vessels disgorged their forces in hurtling assaults. Horses were disembarked and mounted knights thundered through the breaches without resistance.

Mourtzouphlus galloped through the streets trying to rally his men. But the Byzantines, wrote Choniates, "were caught up in a whirlpool of despair and had no ears for his orders or his pleas." Their terror was augmented by rumors of a colossal French knight with a breastplate as huge as a tower, who was said to have put to flight the Emperor's whole entourage. The imperial cavalry lost heart, and even the Varangian Guard laid down its arms. The Emperor fled into the open country, taking with him the wife of Alexius III and her daughter Eudocia, "of whom he was hopelessly enamored," wrote Choniates, "for he was a great lover of women."

In Constantinople the slaughter was fearful. Men, women, children fell indiscriminately to the invaders' swords. "So great was the number of killed and wounded," wrote Villehardouin, "that no man could count them." That night some German crusaders set fire to another part of the scarred city, which burned through the night and the following day.

The next morning Constantinople formally surrendered, and the crusader chiefs turned the city over to the soldiery for three days of wanton looting. Blundering through its streets and mansions, the French and Flemish warriors gaped with barbarian bewilderment at the staggering treasures of the East, then hacked to bits everything they could see. Artistry meant nothing to them, riches everything. "I do not know how to put any order into my account," wrote Choniates bitterly, "nor where to begin, continue or end the story of what these monsters committed. They broke the holy images, beloved of the faithful. They hurled the sacred relics of the martyrs into unmentionable places. They scattered the body and blood of the Savior. These precursors of Antichrist seized the chalices and patens, tore out their precious stones and ornaments, and drank from them."

The soldiers burst into the convents, raped the nuns and stabbed those who resisted. They rifled even the tombs of the Emperors. In the magnificent Sixth Century church of Hagia Sophia, the Vatican of Eastern Christendom, they slashed to bits the great silver altar screen and stripped the precious metals from the furniture and doors. Trains of mules and horses were led into the church to carry away its treasure, and when some of the beasts slipped under their plundered burdens, they were slaughtered where they lay, covering the marble floors with blood and excrement. On the throne of the Patriarch—head of all Eastern Christendom—lolled a drunken prostitute who sang bawdy songs; she then danced obscenely around the church. "Even the Saracens would have been more merciful," wrote Choniates.

After three days' pillage, order was slowly restored in the ravaged city. The amount of booty was staggering (pages 38-43). The crusaders quickly paid their debt to the Venetians; then the two allies divided the remaining sum, about 400,000 silver marks—more than nine times the annual government revenue of the kingdom of England.

It now remained to choose a new Emperor for Byzantium and to partition the Empire itself. The crusader leader, Boniface of Montferrat, was a natural choice as ruler; but he was a longtime ally of Genoa, and the Venetians engineered the election of a man less dangerous to themselves—the easygoing Count Baldwin of Flanders. They also arranged the appointment of a new religious patriarch: the Venetian Tommaso Morosini ("fat as a stuffed pig," declared Choniates). And Dandolo took for Venice three eighths of the city, including the merchants' quarter, where a Venetian governor was soon strutting about in the scarlet buskins that had once been the prerogative of the Emperors of the East.

Most of the chief protagonists in this black drama were soon dead. Within the year the ex-Emperor Mourtzouphlus was blinded by the ex-Emperor Alexius III, with whom he had sought refuge in western Thrace, and later was seized by the crusaders and thrown to his death from a column in Constantinople. Baldwin of Flanders was captured in April 1205 by a combined force of Greeks and Bulgarians, who cut off his hands and feet and then watched him take three days to die. Two years later Boniface of Montferrat was killed in a battle against Bulgarians in western Thrace.

The ancient and indomitable Doge Dandolo, who more than anyone had been responsible for bringing the great civilization of Byzantium to its knees, peacefully closed his sightless eyes in May 1205, 13 months after delivering Constantinople to the crusaders.

As a crusader possession, Constantinople was short-lived; only 57 years later a great-grandson of Alexius III, Michael VIII Paleologus, restored the city to a Byzantine dynasty. But the conquest of 1204 had far-reaching and enduring consequences for Venice. In the dismemberment of the Empire, Dandolo had won some important concessions. In addition to three eighths of the city, he had acquired for the republic the entire western coastland of Greece, plus the port of Gallipoli and the wealthy Thracian city of Adrianople.

Strategically spaced around the coasts of the Aegean and Asia Minor, the ports and islands of the Venetians' rule, including all of the Peloponnesian peninsula and Crete, now lay like a drift of diamonds along the rich seaways of the eastern Mediterranean. Venice had taken firm control of all shipping routes into the Adriatic and beyond. Throughout that region Venetian merchants were to remain preeminent for the next two and a half centuries. Overnight, the little marine republic had become an empire.

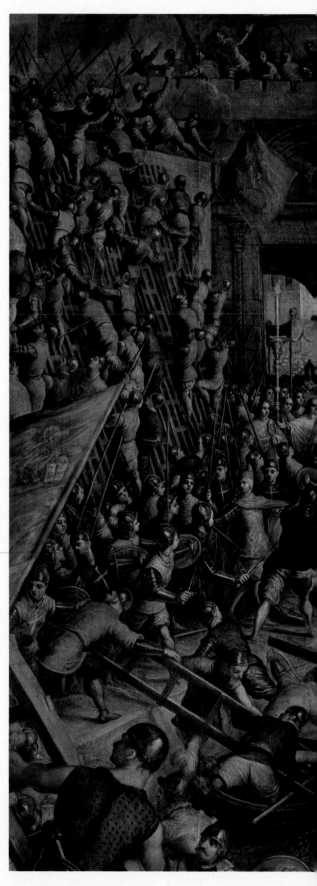

Crusaders from Venetian galleys swarm up the walls of Constantinople while Byzantine clerics emerge from the city to beg for mercy—an imaginative juxtaposition of incidents that occurred over several days during the crusaders' climactic assault on Constantinople in April 1204. So enduring was the memory of the Crusades that Venetian officials commissioned Renaissance artist Jacopo Tintoretto and his son Domenico to paint this picture nearly 400 years after the event.

Glittering booty from Byzantium

Probably no other city in history ever offered plunder like that found by the crusaders when they sacked the capital of Byzantium in 1204. According to the estimate of the Byzantines themselves, Constantinople held fully two thirds of the world's wealth. And it was the Venetians who shrewdly garnered the lion's share.

For 900 years, ever since the Roman Emperor Constantine had moved his seat of government there to be nearer the Empire's thriving eastern provinces, Constantinople had drawn to itself the secular riches and ecclesiastical splendors of the civilized world. The city had held the threads of a far-flung luxury trade that brought in a steady supply of gold, silver, precious stones, silks and furs—all raw material for legions of craftsmen employed by imperial and religious patrons. Successive emperors had also accumulated priceless art treasures from ancient Greece and Rome to grace their capital.

When Constantinople fell, this incomparable heritage was dismembered. What was not stolen or destroyed by the Christian soldiers in three days of pillaging was hauled off to the West, where it enriched nobles and decorated churches and castles throughout Europe. Not the least of the plunder was an abundance of holy relics, the most coveted of medieval treasures. Two heads of John the Baptist were produced (Venice got a tooth), and the Bishop of Soissons returned home with the finger that Doubting Thomas was said to have thrust into the side of Christ. Others divided the corpses of the Apostles, splinters of the true Cross, vials of holy blood and portions of the anatomies of most of the lesser saints.

The Venetians, more sophisticated than their allies, concentrated on items of artistic merit. Their greatest prize was four bronze horses—among the few pieces of classical statuary not smashed by the mob or melted down for the price of the metal—that were taken from Constantinople's Hippodrome and placed atop the façade of St. Mark's Basilica in Venice. Anything else that could conceivably be used to embellish the basilica was also looted: columns, capitals and slabs of marble, enamels, icons, plates and chalices. And a host of reliquaries, ivories, mosaics and illuminated manuscripts found their way back to St. Mark's.

Art historians are unable to pinpoint which Byzantine treasures, other than the famed horses, were brought to Venice as booty; some items were legitimately acquired during the centuries when the two powers were allies. But no matter how the works reached the maritime republic, the result was that only in Venice did much of Byzantium's finest art survive.

An enameled, jewel-encrusted medallion depicting Divine Wisdom in the form of an angel was one of seven such plaques looted from a Byzantine church and used to decorate the gilded altarpiece in St. Mark's Basilica.

A gilded Archangel Michael, flanked by enameled saints, guards Paradise in an 11th Century manuscript cover.

On the 11th Century glass bowl above,
the painted figures—winged genii, nude
athletes and brawny soldiers—
resemble mythological characters but may
be only lighthearted mimicry of
ancient Greek or Roman subjects.

The large chalice at right is carved
from a single chunk of sardonyx, a kind
of onyx. Its gilded rim and base are
decorated with tiny enamels depicting a
host of popular saints, including
Nicephorus (farthest left on the rim), a
Ninth Century patriarch and opponent
of a religious movement to destroy icons.

An enameled miniature of Christ is set in the center of a jeweled alabaster paten, the plate that holds the bread during Communion services.

The four life-sized bronze horses that the Venetians mounted
above the entrance to St. Mark's Basilica had been so cherished
in ancient Rome that they had decorated monuments to three
different emperors before being taken to Constantinople.

A quartet of porphyry warriors, locked for all time in stern embrace outside St. Mark's Basilica, were probably carved in the Fourth Century. They are believed to represent the Roman Emperor Diocletian and the three men who held power with him.

Chapter 2

Commercial lodestar of the Mediterranean

"he wines of Venice sparkle in the glasses of Breton fishermen," wrote the poet Petrarch in the mid-14th Century, "and Venetian honey is tasted in the houses of the Russians." In the poet's time, and for two centuries after, the trade of Venice flourished with a vigor and resilience that no other nation could rival, and its range was extraordinary. Down the Adriatic to the coasts of Syria, Egypt and Barbary, northeastward to the Black Sea and the Crimea, westward to Spain, France, Flanders and England, the republic's ships, with their experienced crews and hard-headed merchants, carved invisible highways over the seas.

The perils of storm and state enemies, together with the number and complexity of trade outlets and an enormous richness of merchandise, gave scope for sudden triumphs and sudden catastrophes. In the 15th Century, at the zenith of Venetian commercial enterprise, hundreds of merchants made their family fortunes within a generation—and many others lost them. Inevitably, the city attracted foreigners. Its business sector, the Rialto, swarmed with Tuscans, Dutch, Jews, Turks and Germans; even German inns sprang up.

The strength of Venice did not lie in the city's own products, although many of these—such as glass, silks, woolens, salt and chemicals—were much in demand. Rather, it lay in the business of fetching and carrying, in knowledge of the markets and in navigational skill. The variety of the goods in which Venice traded invited a ceaseless ingenuity in combinations of voyages. From Germany and Bohemia came precious metals, traveling over the Alps to the south. Ships from Constantinople and Greece brought a multitude of silks; a few were the beautiful finished products of the Byzantine state silk factory, others the work of Greek or Jewish craftsmen, others simply bales of raw silk to be woven into luxury fabrics by the factories of Venice. On these ships, too, came wax, honey, oil, wheat and the sweet wines of the Greek islands; Crete, in particular, produced a wine that was carried along the Atlantic seaboard to the countries of north Europe. From Asia Minor and the Levant came cotton, sugar and indigo, and from Cyprus—a Venetian colony since 1489— more cotton and sugar, along with salt and the rich malmsey wine beloved of the English kings.

But above all, the wealth of Venetian trade depended on the luxuries of the East—that immemorial traffic in spices, silks and perfumes that had entranced the Romans and the conquering barbarians after them. This traffic came by several routes. In the 13th and 14th Centuries, when a united Mongol empire brought stability to central Asia, goods traveled overland from China itself, or were shipped across the Indian Ocean to Ormuz at the mouth of the Persian Gulf, from there to flow across western Persia and northern Syria to the Mediterranean. But the greater route lay along the Red Sea. Indian, Arab and even Chinese merchants would land their treasures at Jiddah, the port of Mecca, and load them onto camel trains many hundreds strong. These caravans would then march north along the Arabian coast to Damascus and the ports of Syria, or pass into Egypt and down the Nile or through the town of Suez to reach Venetian galleys secured in the immense fortified harbor of Muslim Alexandria.

In a scene painted by the artist Vittore Carpaccio, gondoliers ferry passengers on the Grand Canal while merchants crowd the quayside of the Rialto, Venice's commercial district. Here ships unloaded silk, spices, cotton and other valuable cargo, and foreign merchants made business deals in the markets, banking stalls and government offices.

The spices of the East—pepper, nutmegs, cinnamon, ginger, cloves—were prized in a world that knew few other ways of seasoning or preserving its meat; pearls, precious stones and aromatics swelled the exotic trade. In return, the Venetians were able to sell western textiles, the silver and copper of Germany, and—disreputably—slaves. As early as the Ninth Century they had been supplying Slav eunuchs to the courts of the East, and other slaves to the Saracens as soldiers, despite laws that carried penalties of amputation or death. Subsequently, captured Africans were purchased at Alexandria and sold in Europe, and by the 10th Century hundreds of young female slaves, between the ages of 12 and 16, were being imported into Venice from Russia and Asia Minor as prostitutes or concubines.

By the 14th Century the enslavement of the Christian peoples of the Caucasus had become an industry. These races—Georgians, Circassians, Russians—belonged to the Orthodox Church and were considered heretical by western Europeans. They were captured by Tatar raiders, who descended every year in lightning sorties, riding the hardy ponies of the steppes. The Venetians purchased their captives at the mouth of the Don River on the Black Sea, and carried them away, 200 at a

Saintly prestige in a basket of pork

According to a number of medieval chronicles, two Venetian merchants visiting the Egyptian port of Alexandria in the year 828 A.D. heard that local Muslims were threatening to destroy the tomb of Mark the Evangelist, which lay in a church in that city. The merchants, pious men who possessed a keen eye for opportunity, resolved to smuggle the saint to a place where he would be more appreciated: Venice.

Aided by the tomb's Greek custodians, the merchants stole the apostle's mummified body and substituted remains taken from a nearby grave. To evade Muslim customs inspectors, they sneaked the relics onto their ship in a basket packed with pork, the very sight of which offended Muslims. Arriving safely in Venice, the merchants proudly presented their treasure to the Doge, who rewarded them well.

Henceforth, Venetians would claim that Saint Mark was their patron and that Venice was his rightful resting place. Fourteenth Century hagiographers asserted that during his travels Mark had disembarked on a Venetian island, where he heard an angel say, "Peace be unto you, Mark, my Evangelist. On this spot shall your body rest." Local miracles were attributed to the saint. Some writers even described how his spirit chased away a shipful of devils who were heading toward the Venetian lagoon in 1340.

Because these legends were widely accepted throughout Christendom, the cult of Saint Mark brought the city great prestige and political power. The Venetian doges were thought to be invested with the saint's authority, just as the popes in Rome commanded that of Saint Peter, and Venetian traders claimed the cloak of Mark's protection for their ventures wherever they went. In time, Saint Mark came to personify Venice itself. His symbolic representation—a winged lion (right)—adorned every government building, while the angel's salutation became the motto of the republic.

time, in the holds of merchantmen. Some ended up miserably as workers on the Venetian sugar plantations of Cyprus and Crete; others became house slaves in Italy; but most were sold to the Muslim rulers of Egypt and North Africa at handsome profits. The women usually went as concubines, the boys as domestics or as future soldiers. And the fulminations of successive popes were no more effective than the Venetian Senate in discouraging the avid slavers.

Nor was the traffic at this time restricted to the Black Sea, for the Venetians remained ready to trade in human cargo wherever the profits lay. Africa was a rich source of domestic slaves; by 1500 there were 2,000 blacks in Venice alone, sold in the markets for paltry sums. Venetian dealers even bought slaves from the Turks. One such prisoner—a Polish nobleman captured during a battle between Turkey and Poland in the 1440s—regained his liberty, entered government service and emerged years later as a prominent figure in the republic. (His family, it is said, tried to redeem him, but he refused to return.)

Yet the men of Venice were respected by other traders for a certain tough integrity. The cohesion of the little republic, and the mutual trust of its 2,000-odd patrician merchants, made for swift and efficient busi-

Symbol of Venice's might, the Lion of Saint Mark guards the lagoon while displaying the Latin greeting: "Peace be unto you, Mark, my Evangelist."

ness. In the financial quarter of the Rialto, the most complicated deal
could be concluded within a few hours. And Venice was the first city of
medieval Europe to engage in capital investment on a wide scale, com-
mitting public funds to vital industries, the merchant galley fleet, and to
the Arsenal—the great shipbuilding complex that sprawled across the
eastern reaches of the city.

Trade partnerships could be entered into for the duration of one or
many voyages, and were financed by individuals or by a corporation of
merchants. Under the most common early system of credit, called *colle-
ganze*, citizens would back an active, trusted merchant (generally of
moderate means) with a two-thirds investment in his voyage, receiving
three quarters of any profits in return. But by the 14th Century Venetian
investors generally worked through commercial agents resident abroad.
An investor could send instructions to an agent by letter from Venice,
and in return for a percentage of turnover—independent of profit or
loss—the agent would organize the unloading, sale or exchange of merchandise in a foreign port.

As for the ships themselves, the Venetian merchant marine by 1423
numbered roughly 3,300 craft—an incomparable fleet—and out of
a population of a mere 150,000, Venice's 36,000 seamen (some of
them Greek and Dalmatian recruits) made up a substantial proportion
of the republic's work force. Venice not only had created a maritime empire, but had secured for itself widespread monopolies and exemp-
tions in foreign ports.

Most vessels of the republic's merchant fleet, including many lateen-
er caravels—low, light transport craft, perfect for coastal excursions—
were engaged in fishing or in a monotonous trade in grain, oil, wood and
stone along the shores of the Adriatic. But about 35 huge round ships
sailed into international waters, finding their way to England, Egypt or
the Black Sea with bulky cargoes of slaves, grain, cotton or wine.

Just as the long, swift galley was a supreme instrument of war in the
Mediterranean, so the broad, hefty round ship was a natural merchantman. In the 14th and early 15th Centuries the round ship was typically a
single-masted, square-rigged carrier called a cog, which Mediterranean
mariners adopted from northern Europe. With her forecastle and sterncastle curved high above the waves, she moved over the sea like a strange
marine cradle. Weighing 300 tons or more, she was slow and unwieldy
but highly economical, employing only 30-odd sailors and apprentices
plus a handful of bowmen for defense. The cogs generally sailed alone or
in privately arranged flotillas; but in times of danger the Senate might
demand that they increase their armament and move in convoy under a
state-appointed admiral.

The cogs were wonderfully durable. When the 420-ton *Querina* was
hit by a storm in the English Channel in 1431, she was able to ride it out
day after day as she was swept into the Atlantic. Her canvas was ripped
to shreds above her and, when she tried to cast anchor by joining her
three longest cables, she was forced to cut loose again and run before the
wind. Yet she returned in safety to Venice.

By the mid-15th Century the rigging of the round ship had undergone

This exquisitely illuminated manuscript, which was written in 1508, is the first page of Doge Leonardo Loredan's commission to Giovanni Mauro, captain of a Venetian trading expedition. The 30-page commission obliged Mauro to "rule and govern the merchants and the merchandise," to visit specific ports on the Adriatic and Barbary coasts, and to return to Venice by way of Alexandria in order "to load up with spices."

a dramatic transformation. The cumbersome, single-sailed cog was transfigured into a full-rigged, three-masted vessel of romantic elegance and some complexity. These carracks, as they were called, sprouted five, eight or 10 sails—including spritsail, topsail and mizzen-lateen sail. High and stately, they may be seen riding at anchor in the paintings of the Venetian artist Carpaccio. Their mainsails are neatly reefed, their masts fly forked pennants, and the foresails curve and bloom in a wind that leaves untouched the immaculate figures in the foreground. This new rigging lent them great maneuverability. They could tack and sail into the wind far better than a cog could. Their forward square sail, in particular, was invaluable for swinging the ship round as she came into the breeze; aft, her lateen sails helped her beat to windward. All this, perhaps, did not greatly increase her speed, but it rendered her so much more manageable that the round ships could now bustle about in the once-forbidden winter months. At the same time, their high decks became grinning tiers of gunnery that might frighten off even the most courageous pirate.

But until 1514, when they began to participate in the spice trade, these round ships usually carried only heavier and less precious merchandise. The luxury traffic fell to an extraordinary and more famous type of vessel: the great galley. Powered by some 180 oarsmen as well as by a sail, this sturdy merchantman grew from a carrying capacity of only 140 tons belowdecks in the early 14th Century to some 250 tons by the middle of the 15th Century. By that time great galleys stretched to nearly 140 feet in length and, in their speed and maneuverability, resembled the light war galleys of the Venetian state—the *galia sottil (pages 92-94)*. But they were far more capacious as a result of their wider beam and deeper draft. Nevertheless, as single-decked vessels approximately six times as long as they were wide, they were still classic galleys.

By the end of the 15th Century, the great galley carried as many as three lateen sails—with rigging as sophisticated as that of the carrack—and consequently traveled most of the time under sail. In fact, the speed of the galleys was such that in 1509 a convoy of them sailed from Southampton on England's south coast to the heel of Italy—some 2,500 miles—in 31 days.

More important than their speed was their martial prowess. Since they traveled in convoy—often three or four together—and each ship carried a crew of at least 200 men, they were virtually immune from piracy. In the event of attack, the rowers were issued swords and pikes from the ship's hold, and gave a good account of themselves. Indeed, they were more important as guards than as oarsmen; some galley commanders even left most of their oars behind in Venice so they should not be damaged. Only when the ship neared harbor did oars come into use. At these often perilous moments, when a round ship might be forced to hover offshore for days awaiting a favorable wind, only to be blown out to sea again or perhaps even dashed on the rocks, the great galleys would be rowed triumphantly into port.

Nor were the oarsmen the galleys' only defense; each ship also carried some 20 to 30 bowmen (or gunners and harquebusiers after 1486). These

Rowing in groups of three, oarsmen bring a war galley (background) to dock in Venice, while other crew members furl the huge mainsail. The backbone of the Venetian navy, these swift and maneuverable vessels often escorted merchant fleets.

marksmen were selected by public contest. In battle they would take up their stations in the prow and stern or along the central gangway, and they were reinforced by a half-dozen impoverished young noblemen, called bowmen of the quarter-deck, who were serving their apprenticeships on the sea. Little wonder that the great galleys were often called upon to support the war fleet.

The Venetian state was quick to appreciate the extraordinary significance of a merchant ship that was fast and seaworthy and could hold its own against most warships. From soon after their initiation in the early 14th Century until their demise in the 16th Century, the great galleys dominated Venetian trade, carrying the light, expensive merchandise—spices, jewels and textiles—that was the most valuable part of the republic's burgeoning commerce.

Each heavily armed and state-supervised convoy of great galleys was placed under the leadership of a nobleman chosen by the state and carried cargo at rates predetermined by the Senate. The departure of these majestic armadas and their return in time for the Christmas trade fair were the high points of Venice's mercantile year.

By the middle of the 15th Century, the state had become so protective of great galleys that it was forbidden for them to be built anywhere in Venice but in the state-run Arsenal, and then only to the exact and uniform specifications decided upon by the Senate. In the year 1544, for instance, when 12 of these vessels were built in the Arsenal, the legal standard called for a great galley to be 132.5 feet long at deck level and 22.5 feet across the beam—not counting the outrigger, on which the oars were pivoted. Fifteen years later five feet were added to the standard length and half a foot to the beam, but the draft remained constant at nine feet. Considering such rigorous controls on ship construction, it is not surprising that one visitor to Venice near the end of the 15th Century remarked: "Now all galleys of the same size are so much alike in all respects that a man who passes from his own galley to another would hardly find out that he was on another except that the officers and crew of the vessel are different, for Venetian galleys are as like one to another as swallows' nests."

By the late 15th Century these powerful ships were divided among seven great convoys, each charting a separate seaway and each bringing its goods back to Venice for distribution. Most important of these armadas was the Galley of Alexandria (as the Egypt-bound flotilla was called), which sometimes journeyed twice a year, laden with silver bullion and gold coins to exchange for the spices, silks and dyes of the East. The Venetians invested heavily in this prestigious convoy, sometimes to a dangerous extent. Often, after the spring armada had left, the city was short of currency. But the returns were stupendous. Toward the end of the 15th Century the Galley of Alexandria was bringing back 2,500 tons of spices every winter. This treasure would be traded in the tiny but vital confines of the Rialto, then transported over the Brenner Pass to Germany in the spring, or shipped to England and Flanders.

The second eastern convoy, known as the Galley of Beirut, sailed once a year at the end of summer, and garnered the spices that reached the coasts of Syria and Palestine from cities inland. The Galley of Romania

Maritime roads to riches

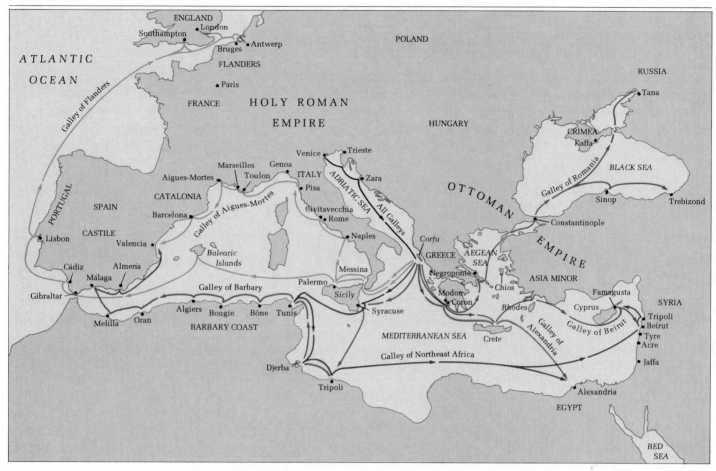

The seven major routes traveled each year by state convoys of Venetian merchant fleets formed a web that reached east to Beirut, northeast to Tana, south to Africa and north to Flanders. In one typical year the cargoes shipped to Beirut and Alexandria alone fetched one million ducats, an amount equal to the republic's annual revenues.

left for Constantinople in late July and crossed the tempestuous Black Sea to the Crimea beyond, dealing in furs and slaves and putting in at Trebizond for the silks of Persia and Armenia. The Galley of Barbary, departing in the spring, traded European silver and textiles in ports along the pirate-infested shores of North Africa, then traveled north to the Moorish kingdom of Granada in Spain. Another African convoy, the Galley of Northeast Africa, ran east along the African coast from Tripoli and then split in two, one unit going to Alexandria and the other to Beirut. During the same season, the Galley of Aigues-Mortes—named for a French Mediterranean port at which she called—moved along the coasts of Italy and southern France as far as Catalonia, selling the Oriental merchandise that had flowed into Venice.

Finally, on the most difficult and enterprising journey of all, the Galley of Flanders, after leaving Venice in July, sailed past Gibraltar and clear out of the Mediterranean world that was so familiar to the Venetians. This intrepid convoy, composed of the newest galleys, visited Cádiz and Lisbon and then voyaged north to sell spices at Southampton. It loaded coarse woolens, amber, lead and tin, then crossed to Flanders to exchange English wool for the linen and serges of Leyden, grosgrain (a heavy, corded silk) from Lille, or the fustians and bombazines that arrived from the towns of Germany and Switzerland.

Convulsive struggle with an Italian rival

Before the Venetians could claim primacy in maritime trade in the Mediterranean, they had to defeat a vigorous competitor located 175 miles across the Italian peninsula: the republic of Genoa, whose merchants had begun to encroach upon Venice's traditional markets in the 12th Century. Although the rivals waged three savage wars between 1257 and 1355, neither could crush the other. It took a fourth war, erupting in 1379 and spreading to the very gates of Venice, to determine whose fleet would rule the seas.

The climactic encounter took place at Chioggia, an islet 15 miles south of Venice, at the entrance to the lagoon. In August 1379, while Genoa's Hungarian and Paduan allies cut off Venice by land, a Genoese fleet of 47 galleys captured Chioggia, thereby blockading Venice by sea. On Chioggia, the Genoese waited for starvation to bring the Venetians to their knees.

Never in the history of the republic had Venice been in graver danger. With part of the fleet, under Admiral Carlo Zeno, away in the East, and the rest of the navy decimated in a recent battle against the Genoese, the Venetians had only six war galleys at their disposal. Doge Andrea Contarini dispatched three ambassadors to Chioggia, seeking a compromise. But the Genoese admiral rejected the offer. "You shall never have peace with the lord of Padua or our republic till we have bridled the bronze horses that stand in your square of Saint Mark," he said. "When we have the reins in our hands, we shall know how to keep them quiet."

Too proud to surrender, the Venetians feverishly prepared for battle. Fortifications were thrown up around the city, and workers toiled night and day in the Arsenal, fitting out 34 war galleys, which were placed under the command of Admiral Vettor Pisani.

A wily old seaman, Pisani knew how to make the best of a bad situation. On December 22, while diversionary forces distracted the Genoese, Pisani's men blockaded the blockaders by sinking barges loaded with stones in the channels linking Chioggia to the Adriatic and the mainland. During the days that followed, the Venetians struggled to prevent the 4,000 Genoese on the island from removing the barriers. Then, on January 1, just as Pisani considered giving up the fight, the sails of Carlo Zeno's 14 galleys appeared on the horizon. Together, Zeno and Pisani tightened the noose around Chioggia, while opening the way for supplies to reach Venice. Almost seven months later the Genoese, near starvation, capitulated. So shattering was the defeat that their republic never fully recovered.

A furious battle between the Venetian and Genoese navies rages off the coast of Sicily in June 1266, during the First Genoese War.

These state-regulated convoys, sailing under the protection of their large crews and of one another, lent a matrix of stability to the otherwise unpredictable 15th Century trade. For even at this time, at the apogee of Venetian power, commerce had its risks. Unexpected gales, the sudden dislocations of war and many other hazards could bring about a man's ruin overnight. Nor were most of the merchant nobles of Venice at this time very rich. They were, on the other hand, energetic, clever and prepared to take chances.

One such merchant, Andrea Barbarigo, has left behind full accounts and ledgers of his voyages. Against the pageant of Venetian history in the early 15th Century, his small drama—a story both commonplace and intriguing—can be followed more clearly than the lives of many greater figures. In his neat, close handwriting, covering page after page of calculated risks, it is possible to glimpse the sudden wealth that could accrue to a man, and the maelstroms that might overtake him. In his way, Andrea Barbarigo represented the vigor and enterprise of Venice at her zenith.

His letters and careful double-entry accounts rarely betray his character. As a young man, he was one among many poorly off patricians who lived by their mercantile intellect. His commercial boldness was probably extravagant even for his time; he was shrewd and secretive, and seems not to have cared much for appearances; but otherwise his personality is an enigma and his private life almost unknown.

Andrea was not related to that powerful branch of the Barbarigo clan that would soon supply two doges to Venice; but he came of an old and aristocratic family that was powerful in Crete. His father, Nicolo Barbarigo, had evidently been a man of importance, for in 1417 the Senate entrusted to him the command of the Galley of Alexandria, the most precious of the city's convoys.

This journey was Nicolo's undoing. While sailing up the coast of Dalmatia on the way back from Egypt, his judgment failed him. All along this shore, barren islands create long straits against the coast that are wracked in winter by a hard north wind. Nicolo, contravening state maritime law, which prohibited navigation by night through the treacherous canals between the isles, pushed on in the darkness. As his fleet emerged into the open sea near Zara it was hit by storm. One of his galleys, laden with spices, ran aground on the little island of Ulbo. Barbarigo was sailing only two galley lengths away, but he seems to have feared for the safety of the rest of his fleet, or simply to have panicked. Ignoring distress flares from the wrecked ship, he sailed on to Venice. There he was arraigned for dereliction of duty and for inhumanity, and was fined 10,000 ducats—a crushing sum.

Impoverished and under the cloud of his father's disgrace, Andrea began his career a few months later. The only money he had was 200 ducats, scraped together by his mother. But the republic made provision for such impecunious youths of the nobility, and Andrea became a bowman of the quarter-deck, attached to the state merchant galleys. Thus he learned about trade and about the sea. He rubbed shoulders with traveling merchants, bartered a little himself, and sailed with the great spice convoy to Alexandria.

Both the rigor and the value of such experience can be felt in the advice of another merchant, Benedetto Sanuto, to his younger brother in the same century. He warned him against incivility to the other young bowmen, against theft on board the galley, and against permitting his servant to open his locker incautiously, lest the wind snatch away his clothes and fling them into the sea. He cautioned him, also, against playing cards and checkers, since this might scandalize his reputation, and finally he put him on his guard against the unwholesome air of Egypt, against the Moors who lingered about the docksides, against disease among the prostitutes of Corfu and Crete and against dining on poisoned quail.

Andrea Barbarigo was presumably exposed to many of these hazards, but little is known of his early voyages. In any event, he soon took advantage of the apprenticeship in law that was open to young nobles of the republic, and he went on to become official attorney in a commercial court. He was 31 before he had accumulated enough capital to give himself over solely to trading.

The opening page of his first surviving ledger indicates that he possessed 1,600 ducats—a useful sum, yet small for a man of his class. (The average income of a nobleman was some 700 ducats a year; that of an oarsman on a war galley, 28 ducats.) But he now invested everything he had—and more. He borrowed heavily. He sold off all his mother's holdings, sublet parts of the mansion in which they lived, and rented a single domestic slave. It was a pitiful showing for one of Venice's older and more prestigious families, but Andrea's common sense outweighed vanity. His borrowings enabled him to rent some storerooms and brought his working capital up to 3,300 ducats. More important, he was well connected. He had rich relatives in Crete and was friendly with the great Venetian banking family of Balbi. And he was wise enough to begin his career cautiously, in humble wares.

From the estates of his cousins in Crete he carried wine, dyes and honey to the Venetians, and he brought back items manufactured in Venice and cloth from Mantua. Cloth was to interest Andrea all his working life, and some of the luxury fabrics of Italy—taffetas, velvets, gold- and silver-threaded silk, high-quality woolens—could bring enormous profits. In return for favors by these Cretan relatives, Andrea went so far as to become the protector of the illegitimate daughter of one of them, a little girl called Marcolina, for whom, after his death, his son provided a dowry.

Then, in 1430, he risked his fortune on two separate fleets bound for Flanders. The greater part of his wares—six loads of pepper—he entrusted to the state-regulated convoy of great galleys. The rest of his goods (nobody knows exactly what) he sent in advance—and at lower rates—aboard one of a flotilla of five cogs.

He watched these fleets depart with trepidation. In 1430 no wars imperiled them, but peace could vanish with dramatic suddenness. And indeed, of the five cogs that left Venice only four arrived at Bruges. The fifth, the *Balba*, was captured by a Genoese corsair—and it was carrying Andrea's cargo. He was not even insured.

Soon afterward the five heavily armed galleys of state carrying his

A sampling of merchandise from the bottom of the sea

While hunting for sponges near the Adriatic islet of Gnalić in September 1967, Yugoslav divers discovered a mysterious relic of the past. More than 80 feet below the surface lay the remains of an ancient merchant ship. Amid the wreckage were two bronze cannon inscribed with the initials of a Venetian foundry and the date 1582. A search of old Venetian insurance records indicated that the vessel may have been the *Gagiana*, a ship that disappeared near Gnalić in 1583.

As intriguing as the question of the ship's identity was the cargo she carried down with her. In addition to nautical equipment and artillery, divers found a dazzling array of luxury goods intended for sale in Eastern markets. Among the salvaged articles were finely crafted ceramics, brass ornaments and more than 2,000 glass objects from the workshops of Murano, a Venetian island community renowned for its delicate glassware.

Cleaned and restored, these artifacts offer a rare view of the commercial culture of Venice in her heyday.

This restored linen shirt was one of three found. Much of the fabric is new, but the intricate gathering at the collar and the seaming and edging are original.

The cloth below, from a 59-yard-long roll of silk damask, was originally purple; rust from its container made it brown. The only full bolt of 16th Century fabric extant, it was probably woven in Lucca, Italy.

Used to protect a merchant's goods, this chest is bound with iron straps and has a tricky locking mechanism. Nearly 39 inches long, it held eight wool berets, the shirts, the damask and a scale.

These were among 40 brass thimbles, in four sizes, that were found in the wreckage.

Wooden-handled shaving razors like the one here had been packed in a chest, sandwiched between slats of wood.

A twin-headed eagle adorns this brass chandelier from Lübeck. The chandelier had been taken apart for shipment.

A scissors-style candle snuffer made of bronze was one of five aboard the ship.

These rusty spectacles, shown with the remains of their wooden box, have leather-covered rims and glass lenses.

This corroded lump was once coils of valuable brass wire.

Multicolored glass beads like these, intended for necklaces, became a Venetian specialty early in the 14th Century.

The two-foot brass rods at left were shipped in this barrel. They probably came from Saxony, a major producer of brass.

Silt darkened the colors of these ceramic plates, which were made in Venice, a center of pottery manufacturing from the 15th to the 18th Century.

Two lion heads decorate the stem of an elegant goblet. More than 700 goblets were discovered in the sea-bottom trove.

The only glass object that completely escaped damage, this bowl is covered with diamond-point engraving, a specialty of the Murano glass industry.

pepper sailed from Venice into the Adriatic, rounded Italy and turned west into the troubled waters of Spain. For Andrea, haunting the business quarters of the Rialto, the pause after the convoy's departure must have been nerve-racking. Even as he worried and waited, the fleet, sailing through Spanish waters, ran into a Castilian squadron of 10 warships supported by 26 other craft. Castile and Venice were at peace, but the Spanish admiral could be counted on to create a disturbance. He demanded to know whether the Venetians were carrying any merchandise from enemies of his king. He must have known that they were, for the Galley of Flanders always took on wares at Sicily, which was hostile to Castile.

It was a tense moment. There were few fleets that could challenge such a powerful flotilla as the Galley of Flanders, which floated more than 1,000 armed men. But the big Castilian squadron had 36 vessels, and they were filled with the cruel and feared Spanish infantry. In the taut silence on that lonely stretch of sea, there hung in the balance the future of many such as Andrea Barbarigo.

But where Venetian strength was not enough, Venetian cunning sufficed. The convoy's admiral sent a gift of glittering jewels to the admiral of the Castilian fleet, who then allowed the convoy to sail on its way. Fifteen days later, safely anchored at Bruges, the Venetian merchants wrote back to their city that they had bought their way out of peril with jewels, most of which had been made of glass. Andrea's pepper was safely delivered to his agents, the Cappello brothers, a wealthy Venetian family with whom he was on intimate terms. Andrea made a handsome profit and by prearrangement his money was at once reinvested. When the returning galleys put in at London and Sandwich, English goods were ordered for Andrea: 23 barrels of tin and pewterware, and 23 measures of cloth. The value of this shipment exceeded the whole of his original investment of 1,600 ducats. But the venture appeared safe enough. He knew that he could sell his tin and pewter in Italy, and although in later years he bought cloth to reexport to the Levant, this time he hoped to resell locally.

But there was no predicting politics. Even while the Galley of Flanders was returning with his wares, war broke out between Venice and the Duke of Milan, who was also ruler of Genoa. The Venetian Senate, realizing that the first act of the Genoese war fleet would be to seize Venetian shipping, rushed a message by frigate to the admiral of the Galley of Flanders, warning him to avoid Sicily and sail straight home. This he did, and in April 1431 Andrea watched with relief as his little fortune was unloaded on the quays of Venice.

By now the whole balance of trade had changed. Commerce with the West was endangered by the war in Europe, but traffic to the East was opening up again. Several years earlier the Sultan of Egypt, ruler of the Muslim Levant, had ordered that exorbitant duties be levied on both spices and cotton—the two staples of Venetian barter with the East— and the Senate had retaliated by forbidding exports to areas under the Sultan's rule and by encouraging merchants to withdraw any funds there. By the spring of 1431 the Sultan's customs revenues were so reduced that he was forced to come to terms with Venice—and once

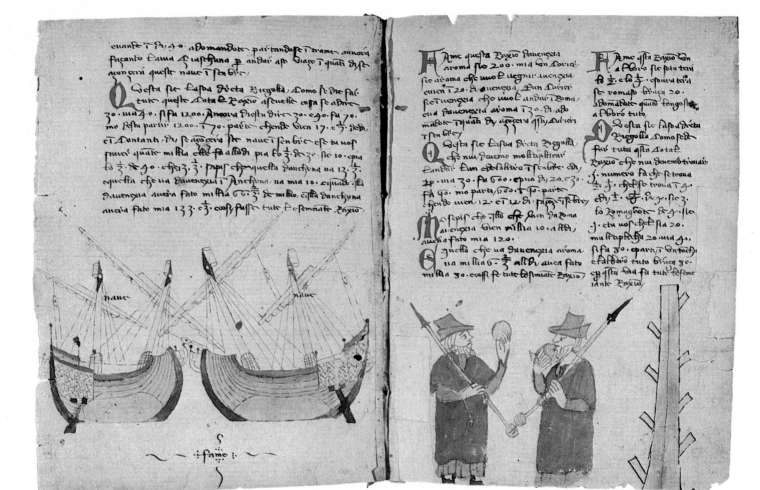

again Venetian bullion flowed East in exchange for spices and cotton.

That July Andrea embarked on his most ambitious venture to date. He bought Florentine cloth, English cloth, canvas, sheepskins and two bags of silver coins of a kind specially minted for the East. This merchandise he planned to sell at Acre, in a market where the Sultan's recent belligerence had almost removed European competition; there too, in exchange for his silver coins, he planned to purchase cotton with little or no rivalry from Italian merchants.

But that autumn was an anxious one for Venice. Because of the roving Genoese, the Senate forbade any shipping to venture beyond the Adriatic without its permission. So Andrea had to load all his wares on state-approved fleets. Some went on the Galley of Beirut, a three-ship flotilla due to sail in September. The rest he consigned to a convoy of cogs, organized and heavily armed by the Senate. With them went his friend and agent, Alberto Dolceto, and they were all destined for Acre, to coincide with the autumn season for loading cotton and spices. It is perhaps a measure of Andrea's concern at this time that he corresponded with Dolceto in a secret code.

On September 23, 1431, the Galley of Beirut sailed for Syria, carrying the silver coins with which Andrea hoped to make a quick purchase of

In the workbook of an anonymous 14th Century Venetian merchant, sketches accompany computations of such practical problems as the time required for journeys to various destinations by ship (left) and on foot (right). Also listed are matters of personal interest, including the Ten Commandments and the medical virtues of rosemary.

cotton. The dangers of the voyage, of course, increased the potential for profit. Many Venetians seem to have shunned it, even though the fleet was completely armed. Andrea directed Dolceto to exchange the silver coins for cotton at Acre as quickly as he could, and to make a return shipment on the same convoy. His letters at this time are full of optimism. "Since there will be only you and Alberto Franco," he wrote, referring to another Venetian agent, "you should, if you make an agreement, have good bargains."

But war was now disrupting the whole Mediterranean, and Andrea's immaculately planned schedules for buying and selling in a market of reduced competition were thrown into chaos. That autumn the Galley of Beirut had hardly left the Adriatic when it was ordered to land its merchandise at Crete and join the Venetian war fleet. Soon, all trade forgotten, it was sailing against the Genoese outpost of Chios, in the Aegean islands, with war galleys of the republic.

Chios was strongly fortified, but it was expected to fall quickly because the main enemy war fleet had already been defeated. Soon after the Venetian galleys had assembled there, they smashed their way into the harbor, captured the seven Genoese merchant ships defending it, and laid siege to the town. But Chios was not to be taken so easily. The Venetian assault became bogged down before a formidable Genoese defense—barricades of heavy merchandise topped with stone that formed a second line behind the city walls. While merchants back in Venice wrung their hands in despair at the delay, every attack was stubbornly repulsed; finally the commander of the Venetian troops was killed, and the fleet's admiral wounded.

From the captured harbor the Venetians looked across at the fiercely entrenched town and did not know what to do. The captains of the diverted merchant ships were complaining openly at their loss of business, and the Genoese seemed prepared to outlast the winter. So on January 18, 1432, the disheartened war fleet raised the siege without orders, and the merchants returned to their buying and selling months behind schedule.

At Acre, when the galleys at last arrived, Dolceto was able to buy cotton for Andrea: 26 bales of it. These he loaded onto cogs that left Syria to go to Venice that spring. Already the enterprise had taken twice as long as expected.

Andrea, meanwhile, was deeply anxious. In June, while the cogs were still at sea, reports came in that the Genoese commander, Piero Spinola, was sailing with a fleet to intercept them. The year before, Spinola's own ship—a colossal 900-ton cog carrying a cargo reputedly worth 100,000 ducats—had been burned by the Venetians in the harbor of Chios, and the admiral was out for revenge. Evading the Venetian fleet sent to attack him, he doubled back to Crete, and there, late in summer, he came upon four Venetian merchant ships separated from their convoy. Once again Andrea Barbarigo was unlucky. Three of the stray ships managed to escape, but the fourth, the cog *Miana*, lagged behind the rest and was overhauled by the Genoese. She contained 10 bales of Andrea's cotton. Of the other ships carrying his merchandise, two—the *Alberegna* and the *Navaier*—also became separated from their convoy and

The ducat—the most trusted and widely used coin in Venetian trade—was minted of about three and a half grams of gold and stamped with sacred images. This specimen shows Saint Mark presenting his standard to the kneeling Francesco Foscari, Doge from 1423 to 1457. Christ is depicted on the other side.

Marco Polo's epochal mercantile catalogue

As swans glide past a gorgeously stylized Venice, Marco Polo sets out with his father and uncle for the court of Kublai Khan. In this time-compressing illustration from a 15th Century edition of Polo's book, the travelers bid farewell to friends on shore (right, center), take boats to their ship (right) and depart under full sail (foreground).

Of all the Venetian merchants of his era, none traveled more widely or with more lasting effect than Marco Polo. His book, *Description of the World*—based on a 24-year odyssey that began in 1271 and took him through the vast Asian empire of Mongol ruler Kublai Khan—aroused Europe's greed for the wealth of the East and influenced exploration and trade for centuries.

The book's impact was due in no small measure to its abundance of detailed commercial information. Although he went to Cathay with his father and uncle on a diplomatic mission for the Pope and then traveled about as the Khan's own emissary, Marco Polo assessed all he observed with a mercantile eye.

He provided figures on the consumption of pepper in Hangchow (9,589 pounds per day) and on the Yangtze River's shipping traffic: a staggering 200,000 vessels a year moving upstream, "without counting those that passed down." In some astonishment he described the paper money issued by the Khan—paper currency was unknown in Europe—with which traders could "buy what they like anywhere in the Empire, while it is also vastly lighter to carry about."

The book's range of information was extraordinary. Polo explained the technique of opening the belly of a Chinese musk deer to obtain the precious substance used in perfume. He told how merchants on the road in Tibet warded off wild beasts at night by burning green cane that exploded in the fire, and how they would be offered young women at every stop, because a Tibetan man was not expected to marry a girl till she had had at least 20 lovers. He warned readers in Europe not to be deceived by what were alleged to be dried pygmies from India; he had discovered that "those little men are manufactured" in Sumatra—from monkeys. "They pluck out all the hair except of the beard and breast and then daub them with saffron until they look like men. But it is all a cheat."

Predictably, ships fascinated him. He warned that some Persian vessels were "very bad and dangerous," being held together by "a kind of yarn" made from coconut husk fibers. But he described with admiration huge four-masted Chinese ships that required a crew of at least 200 men, carried up to 6,000 baskets of pepper, and had "50 or 60 cabins, wherein the merchants abide at their ease." It was on just such a ship that in 1295 Marco Polo began his journey back to Europe and his destiny as a best-selling author and the most famous merchant Venice ever produced.

retreated to Crete when they received news of the capture of the *Miana*.

Ever resilient, Andrea tried to diversify the use of his small remaining capital. He bought a little gold thread in Constantinople and arranged for it to be shipped to Venice on the Galley of Romania. Andrea also planned to transport skins from central Italy overland to Bruges in return for English cloth. But by winter the overland route had been choked off by German hostility.

The new year, 1433, found him almost impoverished. During the previous fall, news had arrived of Genoese privateers looting the eastern Mediterranean. Andrea had received only two bales of his Syrian cotton; the rest was still sheltering unused in Crete. His English cloth could not reach him through Germany. And the Galley of Romania, carrying his gold thread, had lingered to plunder Genoese ships and was delayed off the Dalmatian coast by snow and by the bitter north wind that had been his father's ruin more than 15 years before.

There was little he could do about the cotton and the gold thread. Moreover, Dolceto seems to have been playing him false in Acre, and before the end of the year a curt note had appeared in Andrea's letters to him: "Put your mind on my affairs, I pray you."

Andrea did not stay idle. He now concentrated on getting his English cloth overland from Flanders past the German embargo. For this dangerous operation he needed a trustworthy German to carry the merchandise under his own name. He chose a certain Lorenz Schrench, whom he described to his agents in Bruges, the Cappello brothers, as "a fat man of about 40 who has a thick open beard almost black below and tending to blond above." Schrench signed a statement of indebtedness for the cloth and set off with it on the long journey through the Württemberg forests and up the Rhine toward Venice.

Suddenly, with the new year, the tight knot of Andrea's concerns magically unraveled. In January his surviving bales of cotton arrived at last—14 of the 26 loaded in Acre by Dolceto nearly a year before. Cotton was then scarce because of the war in the Mediterranean, and Andrea sold at the peak of the market. A month later his gold thread came home, and in Bruges and London his skins had been sold well by the Cappello brothers. In April of 1433, peace treaties with Milan and Genoa assured the resumption of a normal cotton trade. And finally, in June, the strangely bearded Schrench arrived with his English cloth at a time when it was fetching a fine price.

Andrea made a small fortune, and he was never broke again. After 1435 he increasingly withdrew from the Syrian marketplace and traded in Spanish wool and oil through more reliable agents than Dolceto. And he prospered. By 1439 he had returned to his old and profitable business in English cloth, working with the Cappello brothers, and the same year he married the Cappellos' sister, Cristina, who brought with her a dowry of 4,000 ducats. The 1440s found him trafficking in cloth, copper, spices, silks and gold with the Galley of Barbary. By this time he had grown independent of his old helpers, the Balbi and Cappello families. He was himself the patron of young men starting their careers on the sea; among his agents he counted Alvise Cadamosto, who was later to explore the

Cape Verde Islands and to nose his ships up the rivers of western Africa.

In 1443 Barbarigo built a little country house at Montebelluna, where the Venetian plain merges gently with the Alps. He began to delegate responsibility for his affairs. And in 1449, at the age of 50, he died, bequeathing a handsome estate of some 15,000 ducats to his widow and two young sons.

Andrea's children, when they came of age, did not emulate their venturesome father. Instead of trade, they invested in real estate. It was more reliable and not as demanding. Andrea, who wanted to keep all his capital at work in commerce, had only rented the handsome palace on the Grand Canal; after his death his family purchased it. The oldest son, Nicolo, in whose hands the family fortune was concentrated, made only one voyage. His wealth was based in land and in government bonds. He died in 1496, expressing the opinion that commerce was a poor investment.

But the Barbarigos continued to be rich. Nicolo's sons became holders

of state office (the oldest was elected a Lord of the Arsenal in 1512) and preserved their patrimony. And the palace on the Grand Canal was renowned for its festivities—those apparently frivolous exhibitions of wealth and high spirits that were in fact a subtle and sometimes useful kind of self-publicity.

From the time of Andrea's father, the unfortunate Nicolo who abandoned a ship of the Galley of Alexandria on the wild Dalmatian coast in 1417, the Barbarigo line had come full circle. Its members were again important servants of the state and campaigners for political prestige. But in this family the commercial vigor and enterprise of an Andrea Barbarigo were never seen again.

Yet the drive, the acumen—even the self-seeking—of men such as Barbarigo bore dazzling fruit. It was through their disseminated wealth that the city of Venice, by the end of the 15th Century, was nourished into its exotic maturity.

Now the medieval township of wooden houses scattered among or-

The port of Modon on the Ionian Sea served the republic of Venice both militarily and commercially. As a heavily fortified outpost, it was one of the "eyes of the republic," keeping watch on the movements of pirates (and, later, the Turks). As a way station along the route to the Levant, it stockpiled spices, raw silk, dyes and wax brought from the East by private merchantmen; state-owned merchant galleys then took the goods the rest of the way to Venice.

chards was scarcely a memory. In its place stood a city of dreamlike beauty—a maze of canals overhung by Gothic palaces, marble bridges, and a whole procession of secretive mansions and churches treading on their own reflections in the water. "The Grand Canal," wrote the French historian Philippe de Commynes in 1494, "is the most beautiful street in the world," and the whole city, viewed from the sea, resembled a fantastic theater set rather than a city of living people. As for the Venetians, "it is their constant boast," wrote a Florentine ambassador in 1463, "that they are the successors of the Romans, and that the sovereignty of the world belongs to them."

It was in the endurance of their government, of their economy and of their political power that such a boast lay. The Great Council—unique in its time—was the envy of Italy. The Venetian system of justice was the most effective and impartial of its day. And the secrecy with which the state was administered, together with the precedence given to age in the republic's councils—doges were generally elected to office in their early 70s—increased the impression that the republic's affairs were run

Flanked by his father and son, a Venetian merchant (foreground, left) entertains visitors at his mainland estate in this illumination from a 16th Century manuscript. Many Venetian businessmen invested in such villas in the Italian countryside, where they hunted, feasted and hired entertainers for amusement. The numbers in the upper left corner refer to manuscript pages.

with a grave and unfaltering serenity. Chronic patrician dissensions, the reluctance of qualified men to accept burdensome state offices (the Great Council was sometimes riven with cries of "Don't elect me!") and the snobberies and petty vanity of some of the aristocracy were a small price to pay for 1,000 years of political stability.

"All the princes of Italy are tyrants," wrote the patrician Bernardo Bembo, "except for the Doge of Venice." The Doge was a salaried government official, hedged about with restrictions; he was not even allowed to leave Venice without permission from the Senate, and his power lay less in law than in the prestige he commanded as the symbol of the republic itself.

The city that had now reached its zenith within this proud tradition was a paradox. Rich, hectic, cosmopolitan, it staged a steady round of banquets and public spectacles that were the talk of Europe. Its young aristocrats dressed in outrageous finery, and it basked in the perpetual sunlight of travelers' eulogies. But, for all its beauty, Venice was ferociously crowded, built on open sewers, plagued by crime, and wracked by winds and rain for much of the year. Most of its patricians lived frugally, and the dress of the middle-aged and elderly was strikingly sober—black gown and black cap. The lives of its women were channeled into predictable paths—they could achieve eminence almost solely as courtesans—and slavery persisted both in households and on the great estates of the empire.

Even the religious life of the citizens was ambiguous. "They wish to appear Christian before the world," wrote Pope Pius II, "but in reality they never think of God and, except for the state, which they regard as a deity, they hold nothing sacred." Yet the pious lay fraternities of Venice, its prelates, its churches and relics—the bodies of more than 50 saints were said to be enshrined in the city—exercised a somber moral counterweight to its proverbial levity.

In most of its faults, perhaps, Venice was typical of the time. But its eminence was all its own. The 15th Century, drawing to a close, found the love of the ancient classical world flowering both in learning and in architecture. But above all it was in painting that the city excelled. The patronage of wealthy patricians, of religious brotherhoods, and of the state itself clothed the walls and ceilings of church and palace with canvases of a prodigious opulence and variety. The radiant, almost sensuous color and light of Venetian painting complemented the weightless façades of Istrian stone that adorned the republic's palaces. Already in this century, the restrained yet magically intense works of Giovanni Bellini and the luminous observation of Carpaccio were predictions of glories to come: the aristocracy of Titian and the grandeur of Tintoretto.

Venice, in fact, gave the impression of mounting to greater and greater heights. "Today the Venetians are the most powerful people on both land and sea," conceded Pius II, "and seem not unfitted for the larger empire to which they aspire."

Yet by the end of the 15th Century such aspirations were doomed, and the whole aspect of the Mediterranean had dramatically changed. For the Turks were spreading westward over the sea.

A seagoing pilgrim's progress

Writing near the end of the 15th Century, the cavalier Santo Brasca, a gentleman from Milan, published a compendium of advice for a traveler planning to make a pilgrimage to the Holy Land. "A man should undertake this voyage solely with the intention of visiting, contemplating and adoring the most Holy Mysteries with a great effusion of tears in order that Jesus may graciously pardon his sins, and not with the intention of seeing the world or from ambition or to be able to boast, 'I have been there' or 'I have seen that.'"

After settling the delicate matter of intent, Brasca went on to enumerate some more practical considerations. Before setting forth, every pilgrim should be sure to draw up his will. He should carry along a sack of about 200 ducats—all of them freshly minted, since the Saracens did not accept worn coins. A warm garment was necessary, and a good many shirts "so as to avoid lice and other unclean things." Finally, the pilgrims should go first to Venice because, as Brasca explained, "from there one can take passage more conveniently than from any other city in the world."

In fact, the Venetians offered pilgrims what may well have been the world's first package tour. Every year two of Venice's largest galleys were reserved for trips to the Holy Land. Each vessel's captain was also its owner, and the traveler paid him a fixed price of 50 ducats or so for round-trip passage, food, transportation by donkey from the port of Jaffa to Jerusalem, and all the numerous duties and tributes exacted by the Saracens from their Christian visitors.

In 1480, the same year that Santo Brasca wrote his instructions, a German monk named Felix Fabri arrived in Venice to embark on the first of two journeys he would make to the Holy Land. Besides being an intrepid traveler, Brother Felix was a meticulous diarist, and his chronicles—excerpted on these pages—offer a rare glimpse of life aboard a Venetian pilgrim galley of the 15th Century.

Brother Felix recommended that, before setting forth, each pilgrim "commit himself to the care of God and next to that of physicians in a moderate degree," for the voyage was long—four to six weeks—and dangerous; disease, shipwreck and attacks by Turks or pirates were a constant threat. "People without experience say that the voyage from Venice to Jaffa is a promenade," Brother Felix wrote. "Oh! Heavens! What melancholy amusement, what a wearisome promenade. With how many miseries is it not strewn!"

In the Piazzetta San Marco, pilgrims cluster around the banners of agents selling passage to the Holy Land on the large galley lying at anchor just offshore. Later, the pilgrims' baggage would be carried out by gondola, along with personal stores of biscuits, wine and Lombardi cheese to augment the regular galley fare ("I'll not speak of the stale bread, biscuits full of worms, and tainted meats," wrote Brother Felix).

While the oarsmen swing the galley onto its course, sailors on one of the great lateen yards shake out a sail. "The wind," Brother Felix remembered of his departure, "was fair enough so that in the space of two hours we had run quite out of sight of land." The captain and pilgrims of high station were berthed in the sterncastle under a canopy, while the common folk slept belowdecks in the large main cabin that ran the length of the vessel. Each oarsman ate, slept and worked at his bench.

*As the captain calls for silence from the sterncastle and holds
aloft an image of the Virgin Mary, pilgrims kneel for one of
the three daily religious services celebrated aboard ship. After
prayers were intoned in Latin, trumpeters sounded the end of the
service. Later, a special service—during which the prayers
were chanted in Italian—was held for the sailors and oarsmen.*

During a stop along the way, thirsty pilgrims hold out cups, pots and bowls for fresh water that the ship's boat is bringing from shore. "The whole galley was exhilarated," said Brother Felix, "and those who before had scarcely been able to breathe now began to sing, for water when drunk after one has been long athirst makes a man as merry as a moderate draft of wine."

Packed into the great cabin, some of the pilgrims nestle in for the night while others argue over space and yet another pulls a bottle of wine from under a floorboard, where it has been cooling in the sand ballast. Cramped conditions produced frequent quarrels. "Monks who are accustomed to sleeping alone in their cells," observed Brother Felix, "find it hard to sleep on shipboard. Many nights I never closed my eyes."

Safely arrived at Jaffa, the pilgrims leap into the ship's boats (left) to be rowed ashore, where, wrote Brother Felix, they knelt to "kiss the sacred earth."

After some delicate negotiations to secure safe conduct from the Saracens, the pilgrims start out on donkeyback for Jerusalem. They were forbidden to carry any weapons, but were escorted along the entire route by armed guards, whose task it was to keep the enthusiastic Christians out of trouble. Though a number of pilgrims complained that they were abused by these guards, Brother Felix recorded affably: "I was so fortunate as never to be ill-treated in any manner by any Saracen. God be praised."

Chapter 3

The great Venetian war machine

In a workshop sign, Saint Joseph, patron of carpenters, points to activities in the Arsenal, the shipyard on which Venice's sea power depended.

n the morning of May 27, 1416, Captain General Pietro Loredan was cruising the Aegean Sea just off the shores of Gallipoli when he came upon an Ottoman fleet of 13 galleys supported by a miscellaneous collection of smaller 20-oared galiots and two-masted brigantines—112 ships in all. The Ottoman Empire, the Muslim power that had been shouldering its way through Asia Minor for the last century, was officially at peace with Venice; and Loredan had brought with him just 15 galleys, with which he was keeping an eye on the Venetians' long-established Eastern trade routes.

"I took the greatest care," he later wrote to the Doge, "to conform to the orders of Your Serenity and to avoid anything that might give offense to the Turks or to suggest that we came as enemies." The Ottoman ships kept their distance, but as the wind died and Loredan approached the shore, a heavy body of Turkish cavalry and infantry came down to the water and loosed off poisoned arrows at the Venetian galleys. Loredan's men answered with several volleys of cannon, inflicting a few casualties, and the Turks retreated.

The next day Loredan detached two galleys from his vanguard and sent them on a peace mission to the mouth of Gallipoli harbor; but they were set upon by some 30 Turkish vessels. Swiftly the Venetian galleys spread their sails, flung out their oars and drew the Turks into the open sea. Then, as a fresh afternoon breeze sprang up in their faces, the two Venetian galleys turned. With the wind and the rest of their fleet behind them, they bore down on their Turkish pursuers, hurling arrows and pouring shot into them. They chased the Turks back to Gallipoli, then anchored for the night just outside the harbor.

At dawn the next day, May 29, 1416, the whole Turkish fleet, fully armed, sallied out of port toward the Venetians. "I at once put my ships in battle array," Loredan reported to the Doge, "and gave them orders to row backward so as to draw the enemy away from his own shores. Then I gave the signal to attack."

His own ship was the first to strike. It rammed the foremost Turkish galley. A ferocious hand-to-hand battle broke out—"the Turks fight like dragons," he wrote—but his men swarmed over the Turkish vessel and hacked most of the Ottoman soldiers to pieces. Now the sea had become a disordered battlefield. Boarding parties ebbed and flowed over the sides of interlocked ships. Loredan was attacked astern by galleys that raked his vessel with javelins and arrows, and he had a struggle to survive. One arrow struck him under the eye and pierced his nose and cheek; another passed clean through his left hand. But "this did not stop me from fighting," he wrote, "for I was resolved to continue to the death. So I ran up my flag on the captured galley, left it in the charge of some of my soldiers and sailed in support of the rest of the fleet." He fought off other ships that attacked him, then rammed and disabled a light galiot and cut down her crew.

Even with a huge numerical superiority, the Turks were no match for the Venetians. As the battle raged on through the afternoon, the Venetians rammed and boarded the enemy vessels until the Turks were all but annihilated. Six galleys and nine galiots fell into Loredan's hands. The

Turkish commander was killed, and almost all his officers, soldiers and sailors died in action.

Among his prisoners, Loredan separated from the Turks all the mercenary sailors who had been fighting for them—Genoese, Catalans, Sicilians and Greeks. These he hanged. One captain, he discovered, was a renegade Venetian subject named Giorgio Calergi; "him I had hacked in pieces on the poop of my galley," Loredan wrote.

The next day Loredan sailed close to Gallipoli and bombarded the city's palace. Nobody came out to do battle, so he burned several more Turkish galiots within sight of the city and retired with his wounded to the island of Tenedos, off the coast of Asia Minor.

In his victory dispatch to the Doge he wrote that "the Turks will not be able to chance themselves on the sea again for a long time, so great have been their losses." And so it was. Of the Ottoman fleet at Gallipoli only one seaworthy galley remained. The rest were either captured or sunk, or were too antiquated to be of use. In this, their first skirmish with the Ottoman Turks, the Venetians had struck a savage blow. For as yet no 15th Century power could match the Venetian war machine—an institution founded on practiced tactics, trained personnel and the finest ships of the day.

The Venetian war galley (pages 92-94) was a ferocious beauty. Maneuvered in battle by the muscle of some 150 oarsmen and driven over the seas by a single lateen-rigged sail, it came from a long ancestry; ever since the time of the ancient Phoenicians, about 700 B.C., such vessels had been supreme in Mediterranean warfare. The Phoenician galley measured some 130 feet in length and had two banks of oars on each side, for which reason it was called a bireme. The Greeks favored a trireme—a galley with three banks of oars—though they may also have experimented with four- and five-banked vessels. After them, the Romans too used the trireme.

By medieval times, the rowers were seated on a single level instead of tiered banks—though methods of rowing varied (page 94). The vessel had acquired wider outriggers that could support the weight of longer oars. Sometime around the beginning of the 14th Century the Venetians adopted the north European invention of the stern rudder (page 87), and narrowed the galley's hull until the ship had become a low, sleek predator of matchless speed and maneuverability. It was about eight times as long as it was wide and was barely seven feet high from the water line to the head of the poop.

The early galley's armament was clumsy: A miniature fortress stood amidships, filled with archers and slingers; and an 18-foot iron-tipped ram extended from the bow to smash an opposing ship. But after the introduction of gunpowder the fortress and the ram were shortened; guns were mounted in the bow and stern, and men with harquebuses—heavy-caliber matchlock guns—reinforced the archers.

But by the 16th Century the Venetian galley had become somewhat overrefined—so long and low that when it sailed to windward its leeward outrigger might drag in the sea and when a light storm blew up, the waves would crash over the sides. The bows were so loaded with artillery that if a following wind sprang up, the forecastle might be buried under the waves. If flanked by hostile craft, the galley's fighters and oarsmen, in exposed positions, could be fatally raked by cannon fire.

Nevertheless, the Venetian galley was the finest warship afloat. Turkish vessels, not quite so lean, were often faster under sail and less vulnerable to storms. But the Venetian galleys were swifter under oar, sometimes capable of up to seven knots.

At the root of Venice's security lay a single extraordinary institution: the Arsenal. Here the galleys were designed, built and fitted out. It was the largest industrial complex in Europe, and by Loredan's time it was already 300 years old.

As early as 1100, when Venice joined the First Crusade, the Venetians realized that their galleys were too important to be left to haphazard care in scattered docks. So they soon coordinated the maintenance of the warships at a water basin situated beside two marshy islands called Zemelle (in Venetian dialect, "twins"), on the eastern fringe of the city.

At its inception the Arsenal occupied a mere eight acres and was more a depot than a building yard. But in the next two centuries its activities advanced from maintenance to building, and in the years 1303 and 1325 its size doubled and doubled again. With the enlargement of the first basin and the addition of another, it came to cover 32 acres.

At such a size, the Arsenal was adequate to the republic's defenses for

more than another century. But in 1470 a Venetian fleet of some 40 galleys cruising in the Aegean was horrified to find the sea covered by a moving forest of Turkish sail—100 war galleys, with more than 200 other ships in support. "If one had heard of it," wrote a galley captain, "one would not have believed such a thing. It was terrible to behold." The Venetians withdrew without damage, but the encounter prompted the republic to extend the Arsenal yet again. When the work was completed, the complex covered some 60 acres; the open-air docks had been turned into ranks of long brick and stone sheds, so that building could continue in all weather (previously the laborers had been laid off in heavy rains and in the heat of the summer). To the north of the twin islands a third basin had been scooped out of the mud flats, so that now a great inland lake fortified with walls and towers gave directly onto the Venetian lagoon. By 1480 the Arsenal provided covered accommodation for the simultaneous construction of 80 galleys; soon afterward the number reached 116.

The days when the Arsenal amounted to a simple open basin were not even a memory. Now it was ringed with windowless walls of pink brick that rose 50 feet above the surrounding canals and ran for two miles in circumference. The complex was redolent of a strange power and secrecy. Its walls were topped by crenelations like half-rotted teeth and were vigilantly patrolled. From the watchtowers, sentries cried out to one another every hour, all night. The single gateway to the sea—just wide enough for the passage of a galley—was controlled by a heavy barrier that swung open on command from watchmen in the towers that flanked it. A magnificent land entrance opened nearby. Above it pranced the symbol of the republic—the Lion of Saint Mark; but whereas on other buildings in the city the sculptured beast held a book open at the legend "Peace be unto you, Mark, my Evangelist," such words were thought inappropriately peaceful for the Arsenal gateway. There, a lion of appalling ferocity held the book shut.

The Arsenal took its name from the Arabic *Dar Sina'a*, meaning "House of Industry," and it was a scene of industry indeed. So diverse, mysterious and unending were its undertakings that the poet Dante, who visited it at the end of the 13th Century, likened it in his *Divine Comedy* to a hell fit for the souls of extortionists to suffer eternal torment in a river of boiling pitch. "As in the Arsenal of the Venetians, in winter," he wrote, "the sticky pitch for calking their unsound vessels is boiling, because they cannot sail then, and instead one builds his ship anew and another plugs the ribs of his that has made many a voyage, one hammers at the prow and another at the stern, this one makes oars, that one twists ropes, another patches jib and mainsail; so, not by fire but by divine art, a thick pitch was boiling there below, which overbulged the bank on every side."

In the Arsenal the galleys were not only shaped but fully equipped and floated. All around its inland basins carpenters and calkers were building hulls, while mast makers and oar makers worked in gigantic halls (the oar makers' room was so big that it was used for meetings of Venice's 2,500-strong Great Council after fire had gutted their chamber in the Doge's palace in 1577). In a factory called the Tana—a huge snake of a

Oar makers hew and plane timbers of beech under the benevolent gaze of Saint Bartholomew, their patron saint, in a 16th Century wooden trade sign that probably hung outside a workshop in the Venice Arsenal. In Venice's heyday, Arsenal workmen kept the republic's galleys outfitted with some 15,000 oars.

An overview of the Arsenal, from a map of Venice drawn in 1500 (inset), reveals the magnitude of the walled-in shipbuilding complex after four centuries of growth. The western basin (left), beyond the gate labeled Arsenal, was the first to be built, in 1104; the central basin, flanked by rows of sheds, was added in 1325, and the northern basin behind it in 1473. Galley construction took place in all three locations. Rope was manufactured in the long building in the southeast corner, while oars, masts and munitions were made in the shops to the right of the canal immediately below the entrance gate.

building more than 1,000 feet in length—ropemakers twisted the finest Bologna hemp fibers into lines and cables of every size. Just to the north of the Tana stood the most fearsome structure in the Arsenal: the arms and munitions factory, which was racked by din and fire. Bronze casters and iron smelters, armorers of blades and breastplates, mixers of gunpowder, brewers of pitch and saltpeter—craftsmen skilled in fashioning every kind of artillery and siege weapon labored here, building and testing the newest and most destructive inventions. Among the designs tried by the Arsenal were some believed to be by the great Leonardo da Vinci; it may have been he who designed a floating battery that Venice put on the Po River about 1480.

The Arsenal reflected most levels of society in the republic. Its supervisory body, the Lords and Commissioners, comprised patricians welltried in service to the state—elderly ex-governors, ex-ambassadors and retired generals. Elected to serve three-year terms, they were required to visit the Arsenal every three days, to inspect every ship returning from a voyage, to report to the Senate on the condition of the fleet every three months and to "see and feel" all rigging and arms aboard all ships twice a year.

Directly beneath the Lords and Commissioners, and responsible for outfitting the galleys, stood the Admiral of the Arsenal. He was a plebeian, it seems, risen from the ranks of the craftsmen; but on state occasions he often rivaled the patricians in the splendor of his dress—a red satin cassock and a cap of violet damask fringed with gold. Pomp followed him even to his death: At his funeral his body was carried through the two doors of St. Mark's Basilica, where four bearers would raise it twice in the air—once in token of the dead man's willingness to accept the responsibilities of his office and once in token of his fulfilling them. The bearers of his body were the Arsenal's four chief foremen, who ranked immediately below him. One was responsible for the carpenters who fashioned the hulls, one for the calkers who nailed down the planks and sealed the seams, one for the makers of masts and rudders, and the last for the makers of oars.

Of all the men who labored in the Arsenal, none was more vital than the foreman of the carpenters. Sometimes called a shipwright, he was in fact a designer who determined the proportions of every ship and shaped the curves, chose the timbers from the forests, and supervised the construction of each vessel built under the axes and chisels of his men. The foremen of the carpenters passed on the secrets of their trade from father to son, forming little dynasties. Several such families became famous. For decades in the 15th and 16th Centuries the position of chief carpenter was held in the family of Bressan, descended from a certain Giovanni Bressan, who had been a private shipwright until 1470, when the state hired him in order to dissuade him from leaving Venice. Another master shipwright was Theodore Baxon; when he died about 1407, leaving no sons, the Arsenal kept eight of his galleys as models for future vessels because he had left no records to explain how he worked. Meanwhile, Venetian officials devoted some 17 years to trying to lure his nephew Nicolò Palopano—known as Nicolò the Greek—from a shipyard at Rhodes. They finally won him for a salary of 200 ducats

The stern rudder: a present from pirates

Like other primitive seafarers, the early inhabitants of the area where Venice later arose conned their galleys with a simple steering oar, which was usually mounted on a boat's right quarter (the word "starboard," for the right-hand side of a vessel, derives from *stéorbord*, Teutonic for "steering board"). In time, the oar was replaced by a proper rudder: a pivoting wooden blade fastened to the ship's side with brackets and fitted with a tiller.

But as Mediterranean craft grew more sophisticated, several drawbacks to this system became apparent. With improved keels, sails and rigging, ships sailed closer to the wind—and when they heeled to port, the starboard rudder lifted clear of the water. Shipwrights dealt with this difficulty by simply adding a port rudder, but there was a more basic problem. Because of the inward curve of the ship's side, a side rudder's mountings provided no support below the water line, so that a large rudder tended to snap off or to tear away its brackets. Because larger ships required larger rudders, this flaw limited the size of the vessels themselves.

A solution to the size limit emerged in northern Europe, probably in the 12th Century: Shipwrights dispensed with side rudders and positioned a single rudder at the stern. Hinged by metal pintles and gudgeons, it was fastened directly to the ship's sternpost—a much stronger design—and stayed in the water no matter how the ship heeled.

The idea was slow to penetrate to the Mediterranean. The Venetians probably first saw the stern rudder in about 1300, mounted on cogs sailed by raiding Basque pirates. At first, Venetian shipwrights, wary of radical innovations, only half adopted the design, supplementing the two side rudders with a third at the stern. But they soon realized the new device was rudder enough, and eliminated the others.

The introduction of the stern rudder led to a quantum jump in ship size: Whereas a typical 13th Century Mediterranean merchant galley could carry only 200 tons, a 15th Century merchantman could carry 600, turning larger profits for merchants. In wartime, these precursors of the man-of-war had unassailably high sides and could support an enormous battery of cannon. So Venetian merchants and warriors alike had good cause to be grateful to the marauding pirates who had sailed in from the north with their steering boards at the stern.

In the 14th Century marble relief at top, a round ship, its flimsy side rudder reinforced with tackles, wallows in a storm. At bottom, a 15th Century relief depicts a high-sided carrack, its rudder fastened securely to the sternpost.

a year (70 more than his uncle had been paid, and at the time a princely income for a plebeian).

The most renowned Venetian designer was not a shipwright at all, nor even a craftsman. Vettor Fausto, on the contrary, was a humanist professor and lecturer in Greek who passionately desired to revive the ancient ship designs of the Greeks and Romans—just as other Renaissance scholars were reviving Greek and Roman forms in architecture and sculpture. "On August 13, 1525," recorded the diarist Marino Sanuto, "Vettor Fausto displayed before the Senate a most beautiful plan for the construction of a galley to be rowed by five oars per bench, instead of the usual three." With almost twice as many oars as the standard Venetian war galley, such a vessel—a quinquireme—would be stronger and faster than any other, Fausto declared.

It was his first formal effort in ship design, and his opponents ridiculed it as both clumsy and unnecessary. But his followers hailed him as a new Archimedes, and his idea was cautiously approved by the Senate, which assigned him a dock at the Arsenal.

For nearly four years the work proceeded. At long last, in May 1529, the mammoth quinquireme, 158 feet long and 20 feet wide, was ready to be tested. With tremendous excitement the whole population of Venice, including the Doge himself, gathered at the waterside one evening to watch the vessel race against a conventional galley, a trireme called the *Cornera*.

The two vessels set out from the Arsenal. As they sped into the lagoon, the trireme eased in front of Fausto's ship; but then, as they drew abreast of the platform where the Doge and the senators sat in state, the quinquireme gathered speed, passed the *Cornera* on the outside and went storming on past St. Mark's Basilica, where a crowd of spectators stood cheering. "It was most beautiful to behold," concluded Sanuto.

After her successful trial, Fausto's quinquireme set out to join the Venetian fleet patrolling at Crete—and soon met disaster. She ran into 14 days of such severe storms that the fleet admiral, Gerolamo de Canal, did not dare hoist the awnings that were normally raised to protect the crew for fear they would catch the wind and capsize the ship. Many of the oarsmen died of exposure in the icy rain, huddled together on their cramped benches.

The great quinquireme was stigmatized as a charnel house. She was soon laid up, and was never duplicated.

Despite the failure of his quinquireme, Fausto continued to serve as a shipwright at the Arsenal and was eventually placed in charge of several docks. By the time of his death in the late 1540s, he had experimented with different numbers and dispositions of oars and had completed at least eight galleys.

As for the lesser-known Arsenal craftsmen—the so-called Arsenalotti—they sometimes numbered as many as 2,000. They too belonged to a privileged class. They were trained in arms as well as in their crafts, and they served as a paramilitary police force, a state guard and even as a fire brigade. After a Doge was elected, the Arsenalotti marched around St. Mark's Square carrying him on a platform on their shoulders. At his

Two shipyard sawyers—one standing on the log and driving the blade from above while the other guides it from below—cut planks in this 13th Century marble relief carved above the central portal of St. Mark's Basilica.

funeral they served as his torchbearers, and before the election of his successor—generally a dangerous interregnum of several days—it was the Arsenalotti who guarded the Ducal Palace.

But they worked always in the shadow of death. Gunpowder was manufactured in the Arsenal, and accidents occurred with horrible frequency. In December 1476, after a spark from a horse's hoof had set off an explosion, the government passed a law stipulating that only unshod horses were to be used at the Arsenal. Another accident, in 1500, prompted the passage of a law forbidding experiments with shells and bombs inside the Arsenal and allowing only the manufacture and storage of gunpowder there.

No measure was foolproof, and when explosions did occur they sometimes put all Venice in peril. In 1509 a whole wall of the Arsenal was blown away. "The stones of the walls fell like rain," wrote the diarist Marino Sanuto, who was attending a session at the Senate and ran out to see what had happened. "I saw many corpses drawn from the ruins, some without heads and some in pieces. They were being brought out on boards," he continued. "The explosion ruined many old houses, but the greatest loss was the death of valiant men." Among those who perished was Francesco Rosso, a carpenters' foreman, "much mourned for the good galleys he made."

The disaster generated rumors that four men had set fire to the Arsenal. Some said the culprits were from Trieste (then a restive Venetian colony) and some that they were French (because the French were frequent enemies). The Archbishop of Crete apparently was among the curious spectators and, "being dressed in French fashion, he was accused and almost put in prison before he was recognized," Sanuto wrote. But the possibility of sabotage was real enough, and all through the night the Council of Ten, a select group of aristocrats who served as the Doge's security agents, interrogated suspects, but to no avail. "Next day the true cause was learned from a half-dead worker," Sanuto concluded. "A spark from a hammer set off the powder."

Another thunderous explosion shook the city on the night of September 13, 1569. "I imagined the Day of Judgment had come," wrote an ailing Venetian nobleman, Francesco Molin, who woke from his sickbed in terror. Beyond his window the sky was filled with flames, and he stared out on an inferno of collapsing roofs, walls splitting open and whole houses disintegrating in fire. "The air itself seemed to be in flames," he wrote, "and I got out of bed only to be covered with stones, beams and debris. When I tried to leave my room, I suffered wounds all over my feet and heard voices imploring help and calling on God."

After "descending the stairs, with my family and my poor father and mother," Molin continued, "I could hardly get out of the door, which lay unhinged but was blocked with stones and rubble. We remained outside in the square of San Francesco until daybreak. Crowds of senators and gentlemen were rushing to the Arsenal, and when I learned from them the terrible nature of the accident I mourned more for the loss and evil done to the public than for our own misfortune."

Only a single canal separated the Molin family's house from the Arsenal, and there the explosion had hurled sentries and lead-covered towers

Calking a galley, a pair of workmen crouch underneath the vessel to hammer tow into the seams, while inside the hull another worker scoops pitch out of a basket for a companion who will use it to seal the tow-stopped seams.

A fiery explosion in the Arsenal's gunpowder warehouse in 1539 rocks the great shipyard and showers Venice with debris. After a second catastrophic explosion in 1569, authorities ordered that gunpowder be stored on two remote islands out in the lagoon—the nearer one three miles from the city.

into the air. The tremors jolted the entire city; hardly a door or window remained intact. The noise was so great that it was heard even in towns far off on the mainland; and the flames, rising and spreading like a terrible cloud, could be seen from more than 60 miles away in the city of Verona.

Besides the constant threat of disaster, the Arsenalotti lived with other hardships. Employment fluctuated sharply, depending on the state of war or peace; many men might suddenly be laid off, and the Lords and Commissioners were often lax about paying wages. Sometimes they fell into arrears by several months. At such times the Arsenalotti could grow dangerous. When a Lord of the Arsenal tried to temporize by giving a partial payment to a group of angry craftsmen in 1501, a carpenter named Antonio di Giovanni threw the money back into his lordship's face. He was forbidden to work at the Arsenal ever again. A more serious incident occurred in 1569, when the Senate decreed that the Arsenalotti should not be paid for Saturday afternoons—because Saturday afternoons were spent queuing for their wages. In a mutinous outburst, 300 men stormed across St. Mark's Square brandishing axes and mallets, burst in on the Doge and demanded their rights. The Doge placated them with gentle talk, but once the dissidents had dispersed the Council of Ten threw their leaders into prison. After six months they were released and returned to work—but with the Saturday ruling left unchanged.

Clearly, the Lords and Commissioners were stricter with the Arsenalotti than with themselves. Discipline was austere, and punishment was meted out by stocks and whippings—and by withholding pay. All workers were required to be at the Arsenal gates when the bells of St. Mark's Basilica tolled at sunrise and remain inside until the bells tolled again in the evening. The paymasters removed from the payroll any employee who was tardy or absent, or who slipped out of the workshop before the evening bell tolled.

The paymasters were also charged with guarding against theft. Before the middle of the 15th Century, Arsenal craftsmen had been permitted to help themselves to wood shavings for their home fires. But so many men abused the custom—taking good timber as well as shavings—that the perquisite was withdrawn. Thereafter, orders repeatedly went out that craftsmen leaving the Arsenal were to carry their coats on their shoulders so that they could conceal nothing, and men caught stealing nails had them tied around their necks and were flogged in procession around the Arsenal.

The paymaster himself was in a difficult position; if he challenged a man, he went in fear of his own life. One city record for February 23, 1568, indicates that a carpenter lay in wait for the paymaster who had docked him; he lurked by a bridge that he knew was on the paymaster's route and almost killed his victim with a blow on the forehead. A reward of 500 lire—more than the poor carpenter would have earned in a year—was offered for his arrest, but the man appears to have fled town and got away.

Inside the Arsenal all work was rigorously inspected and graded. In the rope factory the spinners' bobbins were clearly marked so that the product of each worker could be identified. Removing the marks or

The war galley: defender of the republic

Venice's prime instrument of military might was the war galley, a low-profiled vessel with two means of propulsion: a single sail, and banks of oarsmen pulling on long, slender sweeps that sped the ship across the sea in rhythmic surges like a gigantic water bug. Known as the *galia sottil*, Venetian dialect for "narrow galley," this craft was exceedingly light and sleek. Although the beam of her carvel-built hull was only 17 feet, she stretched to nearly 137 feet in length. Her displacement of 200 tons was considerably less than that of most vessels even half her length, and her draft was only five feet.

Most naval battles of the day were fought at close range and were ultimately decided by hand-to-hand combat. The galley's role was to bring the fighting men crowded on her deck into contact with an enemy galley—ideally in a bow-first assault striking the enemy amidships—and, at the same time, fire a point-blank salvo into her victim. This tactical function was reflected in the vessel's prow: It tapered into a long, spurlike ram heavily reinforced and iron-shod at the tip so that it could drive through an opponent's planking and deep into the hull in one splintering thrust. Spanning the galley's bow, a low superstructure provided a platform from which archers and musketeers could fire down upon the enemy and then leap onto the foe's deck to continue the battle with swords and maces.

Mounted exactly on the center line of the galley's foredeck was an enormous 15-foot-long bowpiece weighing about 5,000 pounds and generally loaded with a murderous charge of scrap metal that was held until the last moment and then delivered at a range of only a few feet. Flanking the main gun were batteries of smaller ordnance: cast-bronze half culverins—narrow-barreled guns that fired iron balls weighing about 12 pounds each—and swivel-mounted cannon. Two post-mounted *moschettes*, breech-loading swivel guns, stood at either side of the stern to repel any boarders attacking from those quarters.

Also at the stern of the ship was a high poop surmounted by a large lantern and enclosed in a wooden framework over which a canopy could be stretched. The galley was steered from this deck with a tiller mortised into a broad crescent-shaped rudder. Here, too, the captain—calling out or using a drum—orchestrated the strokes of the oarsmen. The oars pivoted on outriggers that ran the length of both sides of the vessel, extending about three feet out from the gunwales.

The galley's cruising speed under oar was about three knots. Rowing in shifts, and by a method largely peculiar to Venetian galleys *(page 94)*, her crew could maintain this pace all day. When necessary, they could muster a maximum dash speed of seven knots, with the captain calling about 26 strokes per minute, but even the fittest crew could not continue at such a rate for more than 20 minutes.

Under canvas, with a strong following wind pressing on her single lateen sail, the galley could ramp along at 12 knots. But because of her narrow beam and shallow draft, she worked very poorly into the wind and was exceedingly vulnerable to high seas.

1. LANTERN	9. MAINMAST
2. POOP	10. CENTER-LINE GUN
3. TILLER	11. WEAPON STORE BOX
4. MOSCHETTE	12. ANCHOR
5. OUTRIGGER	13. RAM
6. CANNON	14. FRAME
7. HALF CULVERIN	15. KEEL
8. BOARDING PLATFORM	16. KEELSON

A VENETIAN WAR GALLEY OF 1571

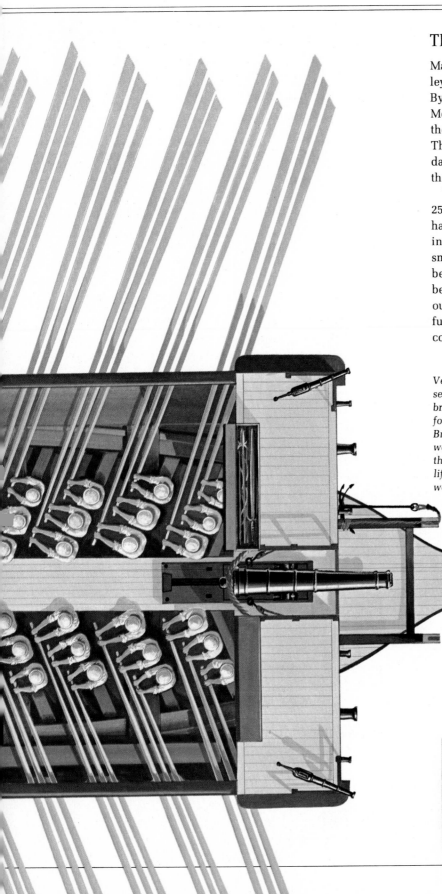

The rowers' arduous art

Manning one of the oars that propelled a Venetian war galley was a task as precise and skilled as it was backbreaking. By the end of the 16th Century, most of the galleys on the Mediterranean were rowed *al scaloccio*, meaning that all the men on a bench worked together pulling a single oar. The Venetians, however, used an alternative system that dated far back into antiquity and was called *alla sensile*, or the "simple way"—although it was anything but simple.

Venetian oarsmen were positioned three to a bench, with 25 benches on each side of the ship. Each of the three men handled a separate oar—a 31- to 33-foot instrument weighing about 120 pounds—and managed, in the remarkably small space allotted him, to pull it in time with the captain's beat without running afoul of the oars of his straining benchmates. Each oar pivoted between tholes set in the outrigger. About two thirds of the oar lay outboard of its fulcrum, and lead weights were inset in the handle as a counterbalance, making the oar somewhat easier to use.

Venetian oarsmen normally rowed from a seated position (left), but when they brought their galley to a sprint they used a footrail set in front of each bench. Bracing themselves on this rail (below), they would stand and then fall back onto the bench, pulling the oars with them. Then, lifting the oar from the water, they would stand again to begin the next stroke.

using another man's spindle could result in flogging or in a 10-year banishment from the craft. It was never forgotten that in a storm a cable might be all that lay between a ship and her destruction. Everything that the Arsenal produced, in fact, was made with extraordinary precision and expertise. All of its manufactures—from canvas to nails—were stamped with the winged lion of the republic and could immediately be identified.

The raw materials too were the finest of their day. Most of the oak used in the hulls came from the forests of the Italian mainland, just to the north of Venice. More oak for ribs, keels and planking, as well as elm for capstans, came from the deep forest of the Istrian peninsula, at the head of the Adriatic. Larch for the bracing timbers and fir for masts and spars came from the Alpine foothills. Beech for oars came all the way from Croatia. Inexplicably, much of the timber was piled in confusion. Even after a special lumberyard had been constructed, the wood was in such disorder that it reputedly cost the Arsenal three times as much to find a log as the log was worth.

Otherwise, the care given these timbers was superb. The oak was soaked in a basin of sea water until it was needed, and it emerged hardened and ready for use. The Genoese—the Venetians' most bitter rivals—attributed the superiority of Venetian galleys not only to the cunning of their craftsmen but to the excellence of these timbers.

In the making of the ships and their fittings, speed was often as vital as quality, and here the great Venetian Arsenal was unique. For Venice, while maintaining an active fleet of only 40 to 60 vessels, could augment it by 100 more with breathtaking speed. According to one estimate, 32 sawyers, 96 carpenters and 96 calkers could build 20 galleys in half a year. But newly made galleys, instead of being put into active service, were sent to dry dock, where they lay unfitted. All galleys were numbered and their parts stockpiled.

In an emergency the ships could be fitted out almost as if they were on a conveyor belt. As the hull left its berth, it floated into the central basin, there to be given its rudders and masts. Then it sailed down the long sea corridor toward the water gate, past warehouses lining either side. "Out came a galley hull towed by a boat," wrote the Spanish traveler Pero Tafur, who witnessed the assembly of a Venetian vessel in 1436, "and from the windows they handed out to them, from one the cordage, from another the bread, from another the arms, and from another the ballistae and mortars, and so from all sides everything that was required." Finally, beyond the gate, where the walls were pierced by a last window, the oars emerged. "In this manner," wrote Tafur, "there came out 10 galleys, fully armed, between the hours of three and nine." Such a tour de force had involved the installation of 500 benches, 500 foot braces, 1,500 oars, 10 sails, 10 masts, 10 rudders, 20 spars, plus cordage, arms, pitch and ironwork, within six hours. Therein lay the real strength of the Venetian war machine.

Marshaled on the sea like an army, war galleys fought by the simple tactics of ramming and boarding. A commander and his officers directed the battle maneuvers from the sterncastle, while from eight to 12 sailors

Venice's spacious Arsenal docks—with sheds measuring 130 by 65 feet—could berth more than 100 galleys at a time. The timbered roofs shielded workmen from sun and rain; the carefully aligned rows of arches let in light from the basin beyond.

controlled the tiller and the rigging. The soldiers stationed themselves both forward and aft: on a low fighting platform in the bow and a higher one in the sterncastle.

Like the Arsenal where it was built, the galley reflected many levels of Venetian society. The captain and his officers came from the nobility; the sailors were generally drawn from the ranks of ships' carpenters and other craftsmen. Until the 16th Century the oarsmen might be mercenaries hired from abroad or conscripted Venetians; in an emergency, one, two or three oarsmen were enrolled by lot out of every 12 able-bodied male commoners in the city, and they were required to serve for as long as a campaign might last. Their wages were contributed by the remaining able-bodied men and amounted to some 52 *piccoli* a day, a paltry sum that represented about a quarter of what an unskilled laborer could make at the Arsenal.

Though they represented different levels of society on land, aboard a 13th Century galley the captain, sailors, soldiers and oarsmen were bound together by a parity of expertise. A sailor might don a leather breastplate and fight as a soldier; an oarsman would snatch up a weapon in support; and from time to time a soldier settled into the oarsman's bench without a grumble.

But that amiable state of affairs did not last. Over the next two centuries tasks became more specialized, and gaps opened between the men who performed them. The mariner's compass was perfected early in the 14th Century, bringing greater complexity in navigation and demanding skills that marked off officers from their men. With the increased power of the crossbow, too, heavier and more elaborate armor was needed. This separated the soldier, who was expected to provide his own equipment, from the oarsman, who needed none.

So the oarsmen sank in status. As they did so, conditions on board became worse, reflecting the contempt in which oarsmen were held. Their wages, it is true, increased and were supplemented by petty trade in times of peace (each man was allowed to take a bundle of possessions with him) and by booty in war. But Venetians became reluctant to serve as oarsmen and began deserting when conscripted. On the eve of the Third Genoese War in the 1350s, Admiral Nicolò Pisani attributed the innumerable ships' desertions to bad rations. But when he tried to persuade the Senate that galley commanders should provide salt pork three days a week, with cheese and sardines on other days, his proposal was rejected—probably because it was too costly.

The problem of desertions became increasingly common as time went on. By the end of the 16th Century, vacancies were being filled by prisoners—both debtors and criminals—who were allowed to commute their sentences to service in the galleys. They had to be manacled to their benches and were required to shave their heads. All dressed alike—in cap, shirt, linen trousers, a tunic reaching to the knees and a coarse cloak—in colors that varied from galley to galley. They were overseen by the galley warden, who rigorously inspected their chains every night, saw to the shaving of their heads and acted as ship's executioner in the event that the captain ordered the death penalty, which he might do in cases of brewing mutiny, fighting or even minor theft.

This marble gargoyle on a wall of the Arsenal was utilitarian as well as decorative: Its gaping mouth fed rope from inside the rope-and-hemp factory to ships being rigged in the nearby canal. The device not only made rigging speedy, it also kept the rope from tangling.

Despite the restrictions upon them, some of the oarsmen were designated volunteers; they were mostly men who had gambled themselves into prison by falling badly into debt. "If it were not for the needs and foolhardiness of many vagabonds," wrote the 17th Century chronicler Pantero Pantera, "and of criminals filled with the worst vices, which betray them into selling themselves, it is doubtful if one single man could be found voluntarily to submit to a life so filled with misery." By day these volunteers were released from their benches to clank about the deck in leg irons, but they were allowed on shore only under strong guard. During their term in the galley they earned a pittance. They received the same food—biscuit, cheese, beans, salt pork and wine—as the sailors; and although their heads were shaved they were allowed mustaches. The captains sometimes set them free to fight, and often they proved formidable.

Other oarsmen, worse off than the so-called volunteers and distinguishable from them by their lack of mustaches, were known as *condannati*, "condemned." Of these, some were men who had been sentenced to hang for crimes that ranged from blasphemy to murder but were instead shunted to the galleys because of the shortage of oarsmen. Others were criminals allowed to exchange their imprisonment for a set term, two years' labor in the galleys being considered equal to five years' imprisonment. But many of these fixed-term oarsmen did not survive to win their freedom. Their spirit seemed to break, whereas those condemned for life were thought, curiously, to respond better. If they were at first treated well, Pantera wrote, they grew used to the work "and then they last a long while."

When not straining at the oars, the condemned oarsmen were responsible for stitching the sails and the clothes of the other men. They were never unshackled until their sentences ended or until they died. And their food rations were the worst on board. During most of the year they were allotted a mere 30 ounces of biscuit a day, with water; in winter and when in port they were allowed bean soup with oil every other day. Compared with this fare, the sailor's ration was a banquet. On only four occasions a year—religious and state festivals—were the condemned granted meat and wine.

Insofar as his chains allowed, every oarsman had a host of minor duties. Those who served on the first bench managed the mooring ropes, moistened the tallow for the oarlocks, and rang the ship's bell morning and night to summon the ship's company to prayer. They also tolled the bell for a death and buried the corpse on land when the ship put into harbor. For such an event other oarsmen formed a curious band of eight trumpeters, "for the comfort and lightness of spirit of those aboard," wrote Pantera.

And well they needed it. Many oarsmen fell into utter lassitude. Others degenerated into a fierce obsession with the petty alleviations and privileges that might still divide one man's lot from another's. But in general they were regarded as cattle.

Yet the galleys powered by these despairing men were now the bastion of Christendom against the sea power that was rising so formidably in the East—the Ottoman Turks.

Challenge from the terrible Turk

In 1499 an ugly little incident occurred at the court of the Ottoman Sultan in Constantinople. The imperial Grand Vizier—the Ottoman prime minister—remarked to the Venetian Ambassador that, although the Doge ceremonially married the sea each year, the true bridegroom in the future would be the Sultan. Nervously the Ambassador replied that the marriage pertained only to the Adriatic. The interchange went no further, but it was a reflection of a change that had already come over the whole eastern Mediterranean: The Turks had become a sea power that even the Venetians had to fear.

When the Ottoman Turks, a nomadic people from the Asian steppes, had first filtered westward in the 13th Century, their battles against the Mongol and Byzantine drew little notice from the Venetians. But all through the 15th Century, while the Venetians were preoccupied with business, the Ottomans were creeping westward over the sea.

In the middle of that century, under the leadership of a Sultan named Mehmed II, they set the stage for the first serious threat to Venice's control of the eastern Mediterranean. Mehmed, even as a young man, was an accomplished scholar, a formidable strategist and a ruthless warrior. In 1453, when he was only 21 years old, he led the Ottoman Turks in the conquest of Constantinople and extinguished the heart of the Byzantine Empire forever. In Constantinople's great harbor, the Golden Horn, the Ottomans acquired an incomparable anchorage, and in their new Byzantine subjects they found an invaluable tool: a people skilled in the ways of the sea.

The Venetians, meanwhile, signed treaties with the Turks and even paid a light tribute so that they would not molest their possessions nor disturb Venice's trade with the East. "Alas! Venetian people," wrote Pope Pius II, "how your ancient character is debased! Too much commerce with the Turk has turned you into the Moslem's friend." But the Venetians' ancient character was much as it had always been. "*Siamo Veneziani, poi Christiani,*" they declared—"We are Venetians first, Christians afterward." And behind the temporary safety of their treaties they enlarged the Arsenal and the war fleet.

War between the Venetians and the Ottomans flared in 1463. The Venetians slowly retreated, giving up bits and pieces of their empire. In 1470 the Turks captured the island of Negroponte, Venice's key base in the Aegean, and the year 1479 saw the fall of the Venetian colony of Scutari, on the Adriatic itself. By then the Turks owned 50 fortifications in Peloponnesian Greece, while the Venetians held out in only 26.

Yet the Venetians were still enormously resilient. After a peace agreement was signed in 1479, they built up their overseas bulwarks once more until they formed not only a chain of marine caravansaries but a loose net that contained and absorbed the ambitions of the Ottomans. Through force or duplicity they obtained new islands in the Aegean—and in 1489 they acquired Cyprus by coercing its Queen, a member of a Venetian noble family, to deed over the island to the republic. Toward the end of the century their trade routes were ceaselessly patrolled by state galleys and heavily armed round ships; their garrisons were at full strength and their dominions at peace.

Sultan Mehmed II, the sagacious progenitor of an Ottoman Empire that became the scourge of the Venetians, was also an enlightened patron of the arts. After exacting tribute from Venice in return for trading rights, the Sultan demanded that the city lend him an artist who would teach European painting techniques to the Turks. Painter Gentile Bellini was dispatched by the Doge and created this portrait of the 48-year-old Mehmed in November 1480, only a year before the Sultan's death.

But in 1499 everything changed. Venice, always ambitious to extend its territory on the mainland, had become deeply embroiled in the feuds among the Italian states—quarrels that constantly involved the great European powers. The republic had been encouraging France to attack Milan and now not only was threatened by the Milanese but also faced a resurgence of the Ottoman Turks over the sea. With war looming on two fronts, public confidence failed. A monetary panic sent all but one of the great Venetian banks crashing into liquidation. Then, in August, the city heard news that was to reecho down the years like the tolling of a funeral bell. Three Portuguese ships, under the command of Vasco da Gama, had put in at Aden and Calcutta, inquiring about the Spice Islands. The seaway to India around the Cape of Good Hope had been discovered. "In this," wrote the Venetian merchant-banker Girolamo Priuli, "I see the ruin of the city of Venice."

In time, seven Portuguese ships, loaded with spices from the East, sailed into Lisbon. "The wisest heads," Priuli wrote, "consider it the worst news we could possibly have." The new route was long and dangerous, but it circumvented both the Venetian and the Muslim middlemen and avoided any grueling overland trek. Soon much of the spice traffic was flowing along the Indian Ocean and up the Atlantic coast of Africa to Portugal. Venetian leaders, driven to desperation, contemplated digging a waterway between the Red Sea and the Nile—anticipating the Suez Canal by almost 400 years—to bring the luxury trade flooding to their doors again. But this remained a dream.

The black year of 1499 never lightened. Above all, it was a year in which Turkish power on the seas became a source of mortal terror. As early as January, a message came from the Venetian embassy in Constantinople stating that corsairs had seized a boat of 200 *botti* (120 tons). But this was a code. In reality it meant that the Turks were mustering an armada of 200 sail in the shipyards of Constantinople. A tempest of rumors surrounded the colossal fleet, but nobody knew its destination. "Many said Syria, others Rhodes," wrote Priuli, "but many others said it would come against the Venetians."

Soon its size was reported in more alarming colors still: It amounted to 260 ships, including 67 war galleys. In Venice a trembling citizenry half persuaded themselves that the fleet was aimed at Rhodes, from which the Knights of Saint John had been plaguing Turkish shipping. As for the republic, it could muster no more than 13 warships. The annual expense of maintaining a galley at sea was equal to the cost of her construction, and many had drifted out of service. During that whole winter the Arsenal flexed its muscles to rebuild the fleet, while the Turkish plans remained unknown.

In April 1499, in an atmosphere of hardening tension, the Venetians chose a fleet commander with wide-ranging powers. Because of the administrative burdens of the position, the man they selected was not an experienced admiral but a wealthy and prestigious merchant, Antonio Grimani. Grimani's patrician father had died when the boy was four years old, and Antonio had paved his own way to riches as a merchant in Syria and Egypt. So astute was his business sense that the whole Rialto kept watch on his movements, ready to buy or sell when he did. ("Mud

Riding in the Hippodrome on a white charger, Sultan Mehmed II takes ceremonial exercise with his courtiers in this illumination from a 16th Century manuscript. After conquering Constantinople, Mehmed and his Turks took every advantage of the city's ancient heritage, including converting the Hippodrome—a sports arena built by the Romans 1,200 years before—into a showcase for royal pageantry.

and dirt became gold at his touch," wrote Priuli.) Grimani had developed into an ambitious, highly intelligent but excessively self-interested man. His war experience was limited to a brief but successful campaign in 1495, during which he had subjugated several of the cities on the coast of Apulia in southeast Italy and had discreetly annexed some of their territories to Venice.

In the course of that campaign Grimani had distinguished himself by his physical courage. During an attack on the walled port of Monopoli, when his round ship was suddenly becalmed, he had headed the assault in a war galley, beaching his vessel immediately under the ramparts and directing his men from there. But now, in 1499, although still tall and imposing, he was 65 years old, and he cherished aspirations less to warfare than to the dogeship.

As reported in the diaries of his contemporary, the garrulous and self-important Senator Marino Sanuto, Grimani contrived his appointment to fleet commander with typical circumspection: "Antonio Grimani asked to be excused for not wishing to propose himself as high commander, but he offered to supply the needs of the state by arming 10 galleys at his own expense." The offer was accepted, and he soon took up a station just outside the Doge's palace, enlisting sailors and marines for the galleys, while in front of him—under the gawking gaze of the city's impoverished populace—rose five hillocks of his own gold coins, with which he was paying the recruits. In addition, he advanced to the state some 20,000 ducats—sufficient dowry for 10 patrician daughters—to accelerate the manning of the rest of the fleet.

At such a time of crisis, Grimani's generous gestures were decisive. The Senate elected him Captain General of the Sea, with authority not only over the fleet but over the whole Venetian maritime empire. Accompanied by the Doge, by the ambassadors of Europe and by the Admiral of the Arsenal, he marched to his galley, which was tied up next to the Ducal Palace, to install a banner consecrated on the altar of St. Mark's Basilica.

By now the Venetians had learned that the Turkish fleet planned to move on toward Venice's strongholds on Corfu and the Greek mainland, and war seemed inevitable. Grimani began in earnest to man and arm the whole fleet, and to gather in Venetian ships from the colonies. On May 2, without fanfare, the fleet sailed out of the Venetian lagoon and began to nose down the Adriatic toward Greece, among whose tawny coasts and islands the duel with the Turks was most likely to be fought. Grimani's forces grew steadily as the Arsenal completed new galleys. By July the fleet under his command was formidable. The war galleys now numbered 44. Heavy merchantmen, bristling with cannon, sailed in their support like floating castles. The twelve great galleys, four giant 1,200-ton round ships crewed by at least 300 men each, 24 other heavy trading vessels (one manned by pilgrims who had volunteered for battle) and 11 light craft brought Grimani's total of ships to 95. And there were more to come—12 vessels still being refurbished in Venice, and many stragglers from the empire. Aboard the ships were some 25,000 soldiers, sailors and oarsmen.

Encouraged by Grimani's optimistic letters to the Venetian Senate, the citizenry back home were confident. The Rialto was frenzied with rumors that intimated victory. But in the Senate, Sanuto and other members of the *savii da mar*, the "wise men of the sea"—state secretaries of marine affairs—anxiously waited for concrete news. The Turkish fleet, meanwhile, had pushed westward out of the Dardanelles—a sinister sign for the Venetians.

As it moved along the coasts of Dalmatia and northern Greece, Grimani's armada took on oarsmen and soldiers from Venetian colonies. Here, from Greek galley slaves who had escaped their Turkish masters, Grimani learned that the Turkish fleet was making its way down the island-scattered coasts of eastern Greece, heading for the Gulf of Lepanto (the present-day Gulf of Corinth), where the Venetian town of Lepanto nestled in a triple girdle of castellated ramparts and ditches. Soon afterward, he received word that a large Turkish army had marched overland and was lying in siege under Lepanto's walls. Clearly the Turkish fleet, carrying cannon and provisions, was not looking for naval battle but was attempting a rendezvous with the land forces to help in the taking of Lepanto. The prize was a worthy one. The fortress-town possessed the best harbor on the gulf, and it would be an ideal base from which to launch raids into the Adriatic.

On August 10 the Venetian Senate heard that the Ottoman fleet was rounding Cape Matapan, the southernmost point of mainland Greece. Already Grimani's ships had glimpsed the enemy sails. The captain general's dispatches, which were sent intermittently by frigate and took as much as four weeks to reach Venice, were still full of confidence. "The Turkish fleet is in poor order," said one report, "and in this we have hope of victory." Grimani's dispatches, in fact, became more grandiloquent and self-assured as action neared. No need to fear for Lepanto, he told the Senate, because the stronghold could not be taken without artillery, and the Turkish artillery was being carried on the fleet that he was about to annihilate.

The Turkish fleet, which was now cruising cautiously northward, hugging the southwestern shoreline of Greece outnumbered Grimani's. The Venetians faced a massive armada of 63 galleys, 30 galiots, 18 round ships, and an assortment of 127 cargo boats and other craft, including two enormous merchantmen that were crammed with the elite corps of soldiers called Janizaries. Altogether, Grimani estimated the enemy manpower at 37,000—with "armament enough to make the whole world tremble," wrote Priuli later—and the mass of their smaller ships darkened the coast for miles.

In Venice, prayers for the fleet were being said in all the churches, and already there were rumors that the Turkish armada was scattered. Grimani, reported the generally caustic Priuli, "seemed to be another Julius Caesar or Alexander."

In fact, far to the south, a strange duel now began. The Venetians awaited the Turks northwest of Cape Matapan, where ragged promontories and little islands are ranged along the Greek coastline. Here, the offshore breezes die in the hot stillness of noon, and winds begin to sweep in from the west. The Venetians, standing to the open sea and shadowing the Turkish fleet as it crawled along the shore, awaited the advantage of

Accompanied by the resident European merchants of Cairo, a red-robed Venetian ambassador discusses trade with the Sultan of Egypt—seated and wearing a huge scallop-shaped turban. Venetian ambassadors negotiated treaties and protected the republic's commercial interests in the conventional ways, but they also organized spy networks, paid lavish bribes and occasionally even commissioned sabotage or assassinations.

these afternoon winds, trusting to the greater weight of many of their ships to smash the hosts of smaller Turkish vessels.

A Venetian squadron commander, Domenico Malipiero—there were three such squadron leaders ranking directly beneath Grimani—recorded how several of the galleys raised makeshift ramparts amidships, and how Grimani, cruising off the island of Sapientza, set up a crucifix for a standard on his ship. "On 24 July," wrote Malipiero, "the Turkish armada proceeded out near Sapientza, and the captain general followed it with all the fleet. Our armada and that of the Turks were five or six miles from each other, and sailed together for four hours, while all the time the republic's soldiers stood to arms." After midday, with the wind quickening astern, the heavy Venetian galleys and round ships closed on the Turks. But the wily Muslim commander, Daud Pasha—once a Grand Vizier to the Sultan—refused to fight, and slipped into the harbor of Porto Longo on the south side of the island.

Sapientza was a place of ill omen for Venice—the Genoese had defeated the republic's fleet there in 1354—and now Grimani could only rage impotently outside the harbor, and wait. Eight days later strong winds blew up from the north. Grimani was forced to abandon the open sea and take shelter beside another island 25 miles to the north. Here, tightly anchored but stationed tactically to windward of the enemy, he waited for the Turkish fleet to break from the harbor. So the strange game of cat-and-mouse continued.

But the mouse was bigger than the cat and was not afraid to move. Soon the Turks had slipped out of the harbor and were creeping along the coast again, this time protected by contingents of Ottoman infantry on shore, who could send boatloads of reinforcements to the ships if necessary. Some of the Turkish vessels ran aground, and many sailors deserted; but the massive fleet kept going.

At last, at dawn on August 12, as the Ottoman armada eased out of the bay of Zonchio (later called Navarino), the two fleets met. On one side the cautious Daud Pasha, assisted by a fierce pirate named Kemal Rais—known to the Venetians as Camali—held his fleet together as tightly as he could. On the other, the Venetian force, now augmented to 123 sail by ships from colonial ports, advanced downwind in imposing formation. Never before had such a variety of vessels—war galleys, great galleys, small galleys called *fragatas*, round ships and other craft—been united under the republic's flag. Tradition called for the heavy and relatively defensible round ships to precede the sleek war galleys into battle and disrupt the enemy formation with their cannon fire. And this was the order that Grimani now employed.

With the wind freshening astern, Grimani gave the command for a mass attack. The war galleys were to advance in back of a thick screen of round ships and great galleys, "just sufficiently far apart from each other," wrote Sanuto, "so that their oars did not clash and break, and so united that no one could make a false move under the pain of punishment by the high command."

But just as the trumpets sounded, up sailed a force of 11 *gripi*—small sail-powered transport vessels—and four carracks under Andrea Loredan, who had left his post as commander of the Venetian forces on Corfu to join in the battle. Taken by surprise and probably jealous of Loredan, who was related to the illustrious naval warrior Pietro Loredan and who himself had a reputation as a dashing and popular commander, Grimani addressed him coldly from the poop of his galley. "Lord Andrea, you did very ill to leave Corfu," he said, "but now that you have come here you may mount whichever ship of the fleet most pleases you, and do your duty like a man." Loredan boarded the 1,200-ton round ship *Pandora*—"a most beautiful boat," wrote Malipiero—while the fleet resounded to cries of "Loredan! Loredan!"

A few years earlier Loredan had hounded the pirate Kemal Rais with a squadron of round ships. Now, scrutinizing the enemy fleet, he thought he saw Kemal's ship. It was larger than the rest, weighing 1,800 tons. The Turks believed this boat to be all but invincible; it was, in fact, not Kemal's, but was commanded by the Ottoman Admiral Borrak Rais, and was packed with 1,000 men, mostly the dreaded Janizaries. These warriors, the most disciplined fighting corps on earth, had been hand-picked as boys from among Christian prisoners of war. Forbidden to marry, they owed allegiance only to the Sultan. They were big men, and in battle, armed with bows and scimitars, they seemed even larger than they were, for they fought in tall, plumed headgear; their advance was preceded by a rattle of kettledrums, and their plunging mustaches and superb physiques lent them an aura of matchless ferocity. Beside this menacing ship, the Venetians now saw another vessel—1,200 tons,

An Ottoman squadron boldly cruises the eastern Mediterranean in this illustration from a manuscript recounting Turkish naval victories in the late 15th Century. Smaller and lighter than Venetian galleys, the Ottoman craft were particularly effective in shallow coastal waters, where their superior maneuverability enabled them to break up the enemy's formation and overwhelm the powerful Venetian ships one by one.

like their own, and filled with 700 men under the command of Kemal.

As soon as the attack was ordered, Loredan in the *Pandora*, with 500 men, and another 1,200-ton round ship, under the command of a state-appointed captain named Alban d'Armer, also with 500 men, steered for the Turkish giant. D'Armer was the first to strike, and Loredan soon after, the ships closing on Borrak Rais from both sides. Kemal's round ship plunged to Borrak's aid, and a horde of smaller Turkish craft circled the Venetians like insects, throwing in a stinging fire. The four big ships, filled with an unprecedented weight of cannon, were enveloped in smoke and in shattering noise, grinding against one another's flanks and spitting flame. The Venetians threw grappling irons over Borrak Rais's vessel and locked it in a death hug, while Loredan, with sword in hand, led his armored myrmidons over the side. "Thus," wrote Malipiero succinctly, "they attacked the great Turkish ship, and continued fighting terribly for about four hours."

Meanwhile—inexplicably—the rest of the Venetian fleet scarcely moved. Grimani's trumpets, sounding the general attack, were answered by almost nobody. In front of the war galleys the curtain of round ships and great galleys hesitated and shuffled—"like enemies and rebels to the state," swore Grimani's naval chaplain furiously. The captain of the round ships, Alvise Marcello, went forward with a few followers in confused formation. He collided with a Venetian great galley, then found himself in the center of the Turkish line, attacked by two big ships. Fire poured on him from all sides. "In the middle of the bombardment," he wrote, "I sent to the bottom a Turkish trading vessel with all its men and seized another that came alongside. My men jumped inside it and cut many Turks to pieces." But by this time the enemy cannon were hitting his ship with colossal 150-pound stones, which even smashed into his cabin. He was wounded in the leg, and two of his staff were killed by the cannon fire.

Then, with the bulk of his flotilla, and followed criminally by almost all of the great galleys, Marcello luffed out to sea. "If those 17 great galleys had only thrown themselves into the fray," Grimani's chaplain later wrote bitterly, "by God, we would have won an immortal victory without a sword blow being struck. The whole armada shouted with one voice, 'Hang them! Hang them!' and by God, that would be no better than they deserved, although if we are to speak of hanging, then four fifths of our force should be strung up. Against the whole enemy armada there fought only eight of our ships."

The little 400-ton *Brocheta* was sent to the bottom by cannon fire (although most of her crewmen were rescued) and the other seven Venetian attackers included not a single war galley: These vessels, exceedingly vulnerable if they did not have the weight of round ships in the van, did not dare advance. Suddenly the variegated Venetian fleet was seen to be shot through with cowardice and incompetence. Officers countermanded each other's orders, or simply refused to move. An example of fighting leadership from Grimani might possibly have saved the day, but it was not forthcoming on this occasion, and the rest of the top commanders—Malipiero among them—were locked in the rear of the fleet by its inflexible formation.

Of the great galleys, only one pressed the attack, striking into the heart of the Turkish fleet. For two hours, surrounded by 60 enemy ships, she fought off all assaults. "Everyone thought she was lost," wrote Malipiero, "for the Turks even hoisted a banner on her; but she defended herself and inflicted great carnage on the enemy; and of our men only 14 were killed, although more than 70 were wounded with arrows. If they had not been so skillful with their cannon, the galley would certainly have been captured."

Meanwhile the 1,200-ton round ships of Loredan and d'Armer, glued to their giant Turkish prey in a storm of smoke and still harassed by Kemal Rais, were managing to gain the upper hand, while the other vessels in the Venetian fleet, dispersed to windward or holding back, drifted like idle spectators. Suddenly, a spark of flame appeared on the enemy ship. Precisely what happened was never determined. To the Venetians it seemed as if Loredan had opened fire and struck the Ottoman store of munitions. But the Turks said that Borrak Rais, despairing of victory, set fire to his own powder supply. The flames spread from the Turkish ship to those of the Venetians. There was no escape. Above the heads of fighting and fleeing soldiers, the ships' sails and rigging burned like paper and the masts were turned to blackened trees before they crashed across the decks.

Soon Borrak's ship and those of Loredan and d'Armer were engulfed in a towering column of fire. The men suffocated, roasted in their armor or leaped into the sea. Neither Loredan nor Borrak Rais was seen again. Loredan, it was said, died in the flames, still clutching the banner of Saint Mark. The rest of the Venetians, motionless, watched in horror, as if at some nightmare fireworks display. "Nor did anyone go to the aid of the unfortunate Alban d'Armer," wrote Malipiero. "Seeing his ship swept by fire together with the others, he climbed into a gondola with one other nobleman, and tried to save himself by reaching our fleet, but he was captured and killed." Only Kemal Rais's 1,200-ton supporting vessel, with the remains of its 700 men, managed to back out of the conflagration, blistered but afloat. The other three ships, still locked together, sank to the bottom of the sea.

Few of the Venetians escaped. "The Turks," wrote Malipiero miserably, "picked up their own men in skiffs and brigantines. For our part, we showed no such mercy."

It had been a day of disgrace—the cowardice of the many only heightened by the valor of the few. Now, in a stronger wind, the Turks withdrew and moved on northward, licking their wounds, while the Venetian fleet, scattered and demoralized, painfully began to reassemble in preparation for a last assault.

In Venice, meanwhile, the rumors were all of a shattering victory. Bonfires were lighted in celebration, and church bells were rung. But the Senate waited in suspense. The dispatches that reached it still emanated from a time well before the battle, and they spoke of little but Turkish depredations on the Greek mainland.

And on the sea, too, there followed a time of waiting. Each fleet seemed to be afraid of the other. The Ottomans hugged the coast ever more tightly, and at the next approach of the Venetians they drew their

A hail of arrows, spears, rocks and burning pitch clogs the air as two Venetian round ships close on a huge Turkish ship (center) at Zonchio in 1499. This tinted woodcut, printed in Venice soon after the battle, correctly identifies the Venetian vessels as those of Andrea Loredan (left) and Alban d'Armer (right). But it mistakenly shows the infamous pirate Kemal Rais —known to Venetians as Camali—commanding the Ottoman ship, which was in fact captained by another Turk, Borrak Rais.

NAVE·DEL·ARMER·

vessels close inshore, where they were protected by land troops, and lashed a large number of them together to form a great floating fortress. Sailing to the north, Grimani waited for them at the island of Zante, near the mouth of the gulf where the Turkish army was lying in siege beneath the walls of Lepanto.

As the days and nights passed, recrimination and disarray among the fleet's leaders deepened the unease of the Venetians. Grimani, it was said, had sent Loredan to his death out of personal jealousy, and his political ambitions prevented him from punishing his disobedient captains, whose patrician families would have made ugly future enemies. Of the second charge he was plainly guilty. He tried to have the captains punished by his subordinates in the high command—the squadron leaders such as Malipiero—but his high command threw the responsibility back at him. The Venetians were further demoralized when Grimani gave instructions that, if the senior staff again disobeyed his commands, their junior officers were to kill them—an unprecedented order that stunned the whole fleet.

At a war council in Zante harbor, Malipiero proposed a change of responsibilities intended to prevent a recurrence of the Zonchio debacle: He offered himself for the perilous forward command of the round ships, provided that one of the other squadron leaders would support him as chief of the great galleys. This move, which would have placed top commanders in the forefront of battle, might have turned the tide of the campaign. But Grimani hesitated. Such appointments would involve the disgrace of men in the high command. The other squadron leaders were silent at the proposal. But later they quietly ordered the council secretary to remove the whole suggestion from the minute books, "so that nobody should be dishonored."

All this time the Turks lay stubbornly at anchor along the Greek coastline east of the island of Zante, protected by their land troops. But the Venetians had now been joined by 22 French vessels (France was Venice's ally at the time). So Grimani's fleet, whatever its morale, was stronger than ever. Against a Turkish armada of almost 260 sail—mostly light troop transports—Grimani could now muster more than 170 ships of his own, including 48 war galleys.

He decided to prize the Turks from their anchorage. On the 20th of August six caravels were unloaded, set on fire and driven toward the Ottoman ships in order to flush them out of the harbor. The Turks, who seemed to have been warned, escaped damage by putting out to sea, and a five-day running fight ensued.

Among the Venetians the displays of valor and cowardice repeated themselves. Again the great galleys balked at attacking. And again Grimani gave no personal lead. At one point a pair of round ships together engaged the whole Turkish host. "They fought valiantly for nearly two hours," wrote Malipiero, "while 40 Turkish galleys attacked these two alone; yet the ships escaped unscathed but for the death of two men and rents in five places. As for the Turks, many were killed, and several galleys were smashed."

But on August 24 the Turks rounded the northwestern shores of the Peloponnesus and at last approached the deep Gulf of Lepanto. The

Venetians and French now had to stop them at all costs, or both Lepanto and the war would be lost. That night, in council, they agreed to advance in the morning on the little port of Papas, where the Turkish ships were sheltering; at the signal of Grimani's guns opening fire, the whole fleet would engage the enemy.

The Turks moved first. In the still dawn they slid out of port and entered the gulf. Desperately the Venetians and French sailed to the attack, but when Grimani gave his signal, only the French commander and the Venetian captain of galleys went forward. The rest of the fleet, disobeying orders, loitered in the open sea. The French were afraid to attack without Venetian support. And the Venetians apparently lost their nerve almost entirely. But as the cannonades of the two lonely assailants rolled despairingly over the sea, a few other ships, including that of the galley captain Polo Calbo, were shamed into following. Watched in silence by the huge, demoralized fleet, they commenced a last, doomed engagement.

"Polo Calbo was the first to strike," reported Malipiero. "The Turks stove in his ship on the right side; three cannon balls from long-range culverins hit the mast, and one the prow; two more pierced the middle of the galley and another smashed into the hold above Calbo's station." Although he was wounded in the foot, Calbo managed to capture two Turkish war galleys, and came through the whole engagement with honor. The others that went forward with Calbo—their names are unknown—captured or sank eight more galleys, slaughtering their crews, without the loss of a single ship.

But looking behind them, this handful of courageous men must have felt their hearts sink. For still the main fleet shrank from the attack. The whole armada was scattered about the sea in disunity. "The French," fumed Malipiero, "discovering so much chaos, did not want to engage either, and seeing our disobedience, said that our fleet was all very fine, but that we had no hope of achieving anything with it." So the Turkish ships sailed on, mauled but still strong, to Lepanto. There the Venetian garrison, craning from towers and walls, watched the sails sharpen on the horizon, and prayed that they were their own. But already an enormous land force hemmed in the stronghold, and the fortifications, although they seemed to be formidable, were crumbling with age. Therefore, when the defenders of Lepanto saw that the fleet was Turkish and that it carried artillery sufficient to pound the walls to pieces, they were quick to surrender.

Watching the Turkish rear guard vanish into the inlet of Lepanto, the Venetians knew the fortress could not hold out. "All good men in the fleet—and there were many," wrote Malipiero, "broke down in tears, and called the captain a traitor, who had not had the spirit to do his duty." The French abandoned the enterprise in disgust, and when the news broke in Venice, Grimani's sons were so afraid their palace would be ransacked by a mob that they emptied it of its furnishings and carried their father's stockpiled spices to the safety of monasteries. The Senate was furious and bewildered. "In four battles not one of our galleys was badly damaged," wrote Sanuto, "two round ships were burned, the *Brocheta* sunk and six caravels used for fire ships. The greatest misfortune

Antonio Grimani, cashiered and exiled to Dalmatia after the Venetian debacle at Zonchio, eventually fled to Rome and orchestrated an astonishing political comeback. Aided by loyal sons and by connections at the papal court, he won readmission to Venice in 1509. Twelve years later Grimani realized his lifelong ambition when he was elected Doge; he sat for this portrait in his regal vestments.

was that 800 men perished from the round ships, with many drowned, and no galley of ours went to help them."

Grimani was ordered to return to Venice immediately, not with his own galley, but in a small vessel, which would symbolize his dishonor. He had anticipated this, and was already on his way back. So the Senate passed a motion that he be required to arrive in chains and present himself for imprisonment and trial. One senator even moved that if Grimani should tie up outside the palace of the Doge in his own galley, as if with honor, he be beheaded within three days. Street urchins all over the city took to chanting: "Antonio Grimani,/Ruin of the Christians,/Failure of the Venetians,/Should be made into dog's beef/For dogs, for lap dogs,/May you and yours perish."

One of Grimani's sons, frightened for his father's safety, hurried to Istria at the head of the Adriatic to forestall his return. There, since nobody else dared do it, he himself fixed the irons to his father's legs. Grimani arrived in Venice in a pilot boat before a jeering populace. Unable to walk in his chains, he had to be lifted up by four servants, who carried him across the quay to prison.

His trial was tedious and unedifying. Nineteen lawyers vied in oratory—one of the prosecutors gave a three-day speech—and the accusations of poor tactics, muddled orders or personal cowardice were tinged and distorted by factional rivalries. Eventually Grimani, rising in his own defense, declared that he had already suffered enough, by now having lain in irons for seven months. With his sons beside him, he threw himself upon his knees before the Senate, imploring mercy on account of his old age. Mercy he received. Instead of being imprisoned, he was banished to Dalmatia.

Slowly, piece by piece, the dense network of Venice's possessions was falling to the Turks, who now ranged close to the mouth of the Adriatic Sea itself—the bride of Venice. By early 1500, while the trial of Grimani droned on, the Senate was combing the city and the mainland for recruits to the fleet. Even the younger gondoliers were conscripted, but the ships remained miserably undermanned.

On July 24, 1500, the bay of Zonchio was again the site of battle and fiasco when a dashing new Venetian commander, Girolamo Contarini, with 34 war galleys, 13 great galleys and 20 round ships, attacked a Turkish fleet of 230 sail. Much of his small armada virtually deserted the field when his own ship, struck by cannon fire, began to sink; and two great galleys fell into the hands of the enemy.

Marveling at the size of the mammoth vessels, the Turks scuttled one but sailed the other back to Constantinople. There the Sultan ordered the construction of 50 ships like it, but the Turkish foremen ashamedly admitted that this could scarcely be done; the work of the Venetians was so skillful that it was almost impossible to duplicate. The old shipbuilding traditions of Venice remained secure, it seems, even though the ancient valor was gone.

By the end of the year, having lost almost all her possessions on the Greek mainland, Venice entrusted her hopes to a new Captain General of the Sea. This man, Benedetto Pesaro, was an insatiable libertine (it was

A pair of Ottoman galleys lie at anchor beneath the guns of Coron, one of several Ionian ports the Turks seized from the Venetians during a summer campaign in 1500. The conquests, coming only a year after the Turks' stunning victory at Zonchio, ensured continued Ottoman control of the eastern Mediterranean.

disgusting, wrote Priuli, that Pesaro should still be enjoying mistresses at the age of 70). He was also experienced in warfare, vigorous, taciturn, and knew the mind of his men. He partially solved the problem of recruitment by promising his crews plunder, which made war service infinitely more rewarding. Nor was he afraid of Venice's powerful families, as Grimani had been. When two nobles—one from the great family of Loredan—surrendered their forts to the Turks against his orders, he simply beheaded them.

By 1502 Benedetto Pesaro's force had recaptured two of the Venetians' Greek outposts and had prowled into the Gulf of Arta in western Greece—where the Turks were constructing ships—smashing or seizing everything along his way. It was typical of Pesaro that when he captured the Turkish corsair Enrichi, who had once roasted to death a Venetian nobleman, he roasted the prisoner to avenge the nobleman—very thoroughly, for three hours.

But Pesaro's ruthless prosecution of the war was not sufficient to restore Venice to its former power, and by the time he died in August 1503, Venice had signed a humiliating peace. The treaty confirmed the Turks in their tenure of almost all mainland Greece. And within a few years the balance of power in the Mediterranean shifted even more dramatically. In 1516 the Turks seized Syria and Palestine, almost liquidating the old Mamluk Empire at the Battle of Mark Dabik, where the Egyptian Sultan Kansou fell dead of apoplexy in the field. By January 1517 Egypt itself had fallen to the Ottomans.

Soon the Turks had formed alliances with their coreligionists, the Barbary corsairs of North Africa—Berbers, renegades and Levantine adventurers who ruled piratical petty states along the shallow harbors and lagoons of the North African coast. The corsairs supplied many of the most experienced admirals and toughest crews in the Ottoman fleet. Ferociously turbaned and mustached, their sashes stuck with sabers and daggers, they lived by plunder and the slave trade, and became the terror of the Christian world.

Khair-ed-Din Barbarossa especially—the terrible and sagacious Red Beard, who appointed himself ruler of Algiers and later served as high admiral of the Ottoman fleet—scourged the Christian coasts of the Mediterranean for two decades before he died in his bed in 1546. Later the corsair Turgut Rais—"the Drawn Sword of Islam," as Muslim chroniclers hailed him—followed in his stead as a name that Christian parents used to frighten their naughty children. A ferocious former prisoner of the Christians (he had once toiled in chains in a Genoese galley), Turgut sailed year after year from his lair in a secret inlet in Tunisia to terrorize Christian shipping.

Against such threats the thin, perforated net of the Venetians' defenses survived chiefly by means of diplomacy at Constantinople, where Venetian ambassadors bribed officials of the Ottoman empire into sympathizing with the republic. The Venetians, in fact, were the foreigners most popular with the Turks, for they brought the richest gifts. But the West, consequently, was suspicious of Venice as an ally; the Christians failed to unite, and they lost their hold on the Mediterranean with terrifying suddenness. By 1530, encircling all Mediterranean waters except for the

Adriatic, the Sultan had indeed become the bridegroom of the sea.

For Venice the early 16th Century was a time of crisis. War, the decline of the spice trade and recurring epidemic diseases all played on the nerves of a city whose inner strength was ebbing away. In 1509, at Agnadello on the Italian mainland, the Venetian army was broken by the combined forces of Spain, France, the papacy, the Holy Roman Empire and a miscellany of Italian states. These powers, many of them erstwhile allies of Venice, had turned on the city out of greed for its territory. They even reached the edge of the lagoon. But Venice exploited the disunity of the invaders, and its mainland peasantry rose against them, so that by 1517 the republic had regained almost all its Italian territory. Nevertheless, the Venetians were deeply shaken.

Other factors were exacerbating the decline. The nobles were turning from trade to speculation in real estate. Industry and banking were proving safer and more profitable than commerce, and there was slowly arising that profligate and luxury-loving Venice, the city of theater and carnivals, that would dazzle or disgust later centuries. Courtesans displayed themselves freely, sporting yellow hair and painted bosoms. (Even the pompous and conservative Sanuto sired two illegitimate daughters.) Gambling and begging increased. Syphilis spread. The sermons of friars turned angrily on wigs and hairpieces, sensual books and pictures, and when the Senate banned extravagant public dress, the citizens slashed their sleeves to show off glittering undergarments.

As for the fleet, the problem of recruitment remained paramount. "The people are so comfortable and well-to-do," wrote Admiral Cristoforo da Canale in 1539, "that nothing less than overwhelming need would induce them to embark in a galley." By the end of the century most of the oarsmen were convicts or debtors, and many of the captains—who had jockeyed for their appointments by influence or bribery in the Senate—were noblemen of little experience. Swathed in ermine, silk, even cloth of gold, they bestrode the poops of their overgilded galleys like pampered idols, while beneath them the manacled rowers heaved and sweated and died, as disregarded as dogs.

Yet the Arsenal was still a prodigious factory, and the Venetians' pride and resilience, if not their strength, remained unquenched. By midcentury, Venetian agricultural estates on the mainland and in overseas territories were flourishing as never before, and with the failure of the Portuguese to monopolize the Eastern trade routes, the spice trade revived. In particular the jewel of the republic's dwindling empire, the island of Cyprus, poured a rich revenue into the city in the forms of salt, sugar, cotton, wax, honey, indigo, saffron and wine. The Venetians, in fact, milked Cyprus' Greek populace unmercifully. "There is yearly some tax or other imposed on them," wrote the German traveler Martin von Baumgarten, "with which the poor common people are so flayed and pillaged that they hardly have the wherewithal to keep soul and body together." And now this island attracted the avarice of the Turk.

It is strange that the War of Cyprus, as it is called, was not precipitated earlier by the Turks, for the rich island was so close to their shores that on a clear day it was visible over the sea. In any event, the winter of

Tools of the sea warriors' trade

When Venetian and Turkish war galleys surged toward each other for the bloody close-quarters combat that climaxed most 16th Century sea battles, the personal arms and armor of the warriors who were huddled behind the bulwarks became as important to the outcome as the agility of the ships or the havoc inflicted by the booming cannon.

The Venetians depended on hand-held firearms during the approach, but the range and accuracy of their primitive harquebuses and pistols were sorely limited. At any appreciable distance the Turks held an advantage in their archers armed with the great composite bow. Its glued-together layers of wood, bone and sinew fibers gave this weapon immense power. Expert Turkish archers could fling volleys of arrows across 500 yards of water, penetrate armor at up to 100 yards, and shoot more accurately and rapidly than the Venetians could with their weapons.

As the vessels drew closer, the advantage shifted. Whereas Venetians could easily fire their small arms while crouching behind cover, Turkish archers usually had to stand up straight to draw their bows, exposing themselves to enemy shots.

The decisive moment came as the galleys crashed together and the soldiers of each side tried to board the enemy ship. Now the striking weapons—swords and maces—played their role, and body armor was of great importance. A typical European warrior went into battle plated from his helmet to the tasses on his upper thighs, while his Turkish counterpart rarely wore more than a meshlike covering of chain mail. The Muslim's lighter, more flexible armor afforded him easier movement—but much less protection.

The balance of the various elements in this martial equation would change in the latter part of the 16th Century: Western firearms improved, and the Turks found themselves hard-pressed to keep their highly trained corps of archers up to strength. But while the Turks still had plenty of bowmen, a naval engagement of roughly equal forces was anybody's fight.

The intricate engraving suggests that the 16th Century Italian half-armor and helmet at near right belonged to an officer. The 16th Century Turkish armor at far right is made of riveted iron links. Although the helmet is not much more than a skullcap, it has hanging mail to protect the back of the warrior's neck. Two rows of iron lames—overlapping plates—protect the fighter's vital organs.

118

This Turkish shield is woven of cane rings bound by colored silk threads, with a fluted plate of steel at its center.

Decorations of turquoise and inlaid gold indicate that the yard-long cutlass above—pictured with a scabbard that was once covered with velvet—was the property of a wealthy Turkish officer. The blade is double-edged near the point and bears a Persian inscription with advice to landlubbers: "If you seek security, stay on shore."

Grasped from behind by a riveted crossbar, this steel buckler bears a Venetian family coat of arms (bottom) and the republic's Lion of Saint Mark (top).

This four-pound Venetian mace bristles with deadly flanges.

A Western European wheel-lock pistol produced a spark to fire the powder—a great improvement over earlier models, which required lighting a fuse.

This iron flask carried charge powder for a Venetian harquebus, a matchlock gun. The harquebusier slung it from his belt or shoulder by its tasseled silk cord.

Turks could fire six arrows per minute with a composite bow like this one— shown unstrung beside its carrying case, which was made of leather and canvas.

1569-1570—one of the most tempestuous Mediterranean winters on record—brought disturbing reports that the Turks were furiously arming again. All through Europe the familiar guessing began: At what target would the Turkish armament be aimed?

In January 1570 the Turks confiscated two Venetian cargo ships that were in Constantinople. Finally, in March 1570, Sultan Selim II—known as "Selim the Sot" because of his addiction to wine—peremptorily demanded that Venice cede him the island of Cyprus. "Selim, Ottoman Sultan," he began, "Emperor of the Turks, Lord of Lords, King of Kings, Shadow of God, Lord of the Earthly Paradise of Jerusalem, to the Signory of Venice: We demand of you Cyprus, which you shall give us willingly or perforce; and do you not irritate our horrible sword, for we shall wage most cruel war against you everywhere; nor let you trust in your treasure, for we shall cause it suddenly to run away from you like a torrent; beware to irritate us."

One story has it that the drink-sodden Selim coveted the island for its wine; it is more likely that the Sultan was incensed because Cyprus gave safe harbor to Christian pirates, and was attracted by the vulnerability and abundance of the island. But in answer to his demand the Venetian Senate replied with dignity that Venice was the legitimate mistress of Cyprus, and that by the grace of Christ the republic would possess the courage to defend it.

Venice appealed to the West, and a vigorous new Pope, Pius V, sent out calls for assistance even to the Persians and Russians, the Ottoman Empire's old neighbors and enemies to the north and east. But it was King Philip II of Spain who, although he was reluctant to become involved and suspicious of the Venetians' motives, finally came to the aid of the republic—"out of zeal for religion, though at great inconvenience," he said—for Spain too was starting to be fearful of the Turkish threat. Thus an unofficial Holy League was formed, allying the Christian trio of Venice, the papacy and Spain.

During three decades of peace the Venetian battle fleet had stagnated, but soon, once again, reserve galleys were pushing out of the Arsenal. A colossal quadrireme constructed by the scholar-turned-shipwright Vettor Fausto was loaded with batteries of cannon. On March 31, 1570, the Venetian captain general, Girolamo Zane, a heavy-jowled sea dog with a walrus mustache and an expression of black-eyed intemperance, sailed from the city with a fleet of 42 galleys, picked up another 30 Venetian vessels at sea and awaited his Spanish and papal allies at Zara on the Dalmatian shore of the Adriatic. He remained there for two months during which a virulent disease killed thousands of his men, and still his allies did not come.

Pitifully undermanned and short of provisions, Zane limped on to Corfu, where he hoped to be able to replenish his fleet. But the island yielded almost nothing, and he continued on to Crete. There, other Venetian vessels increased his fleet to 144, but he was still desperately short of men. On August 31, when 49 Spanish galleys arrived in Crete in company with a little papal squadron of 12 galleys bearing the commander of the fleet, Marc Antonio Colonna, the Venetian inferiority in manpower became blatantly apparent.

At the first review of the fleet, the Venetians, instead of standing out to sea, where their strength or weakness would be obvious to their allies, lined up their ships in the harbor, poops to shore. The commander of the Spanish contingent, Gian Andrea Doria, said they did this so that men could be transferred covertly from galley to galley, confusing estimation of their strength. Angry arguments broke out among the commanders. Zane and Colonna wanted to press on to the relief of Cyprus, but Doria procrastinated, pleading the lateness of the season and the feebleness of the Venetians. For days the admirals wrangled, until Zane and Doria no longer spoke to each other.

Meanwhile, in late June, the Turks, under their commander, Piale Pasha, had sailed for Cyprus with a fleet of 350 ships, and had surged over the island, capturing every strong point except Nicosia and the great fortified port of Famagusta. On September 9, Nicosia too fell. More than 20,000 of its population were put to the sword, and 15,000 more taken prisoner. "The victors kept cutting off the heads of old women," wrote Angelo Calepio, a Dominican superior who was present; "to prove their swords, many of them as they marched along split open the heads of men who had already surrendered. Did a prisoner try to escape, he was caught up and his legs cut off, and as long as any life was left in him every Janizary who passed had a cut at him. Among the slain were

123

A 16th Century allegorical painting dramatizes Venetian preparations for one of the republic's frequent campaigns against the Ottoman Empire. At left, three provveditori, or commissioners of the Arsenal, confer with Saint Mark, patron of the republic (far left), and enlist the armored figure of Mars, Roman god of war. At right, the Doge, accompanied by his court, inspects the anchored war fleet.

Lodovico Podochatoro and Lucretia Calepia, my mother, whose head they cut off on her serving maid's lap."

The commander of the Turkish land forces, Lala Mustapha, selected the most beautiful female captives and loaded them onto a ship that was destined for the harem of Sultan Selim, but one of the women, in despair, set fire to the vessel's powder magazine and blew herself and her companions into the sea.

News of the fall of Nicosia reached the allied fleet on September 21 as it cruised indecisively off the southern coast of Turkey. After further arguments, Doria finally turned for home, and the whole expedition foundered. Storms swept the retreating ships, wrecking 11 of the Venetian galleys. Colonna's flotilla was reduced to a derisory three vessels when it took a beating from 18 Turkish galleys it met on October 26. The Holy League appeared to have dissolved almost before its inception.

Venice, as ever, was cruel to her failed servants. Zane was condemned to prison, where he soon died, and the punishments of the Senate reached down even to subalterns. The naval might of the republic, it seemed—her courage, her expertise—was irretrievably gone.

Yet in less than a year Venice was to show that she was not dead, but sleeping, for she would challenge the Turk's grip on the Mediterranean in one of the greatest sea battles ever fought.

An exotic society rooted in slavery

As the Christian nations of 16th Century Europe battled the Ottoman Empire, they were continually astonished by the alien ways of this upstart power—particularly its political system. The Turks, whose might had made them rulers of a dominion stretching from Greece and Hungary to North Africa, were utterly subservient to one despotic warlord. "No one ever dreamed of such a tyranny," marveled a Venetian ambassador. The Sultan "puts his subjects to death at will, and they accept their fate without resistance."

To lessen the danger of plots, the Sultan actually owned those responsible for carrying out his desires: The civil government, the military command and the 20,000-person court were staffed by slaves—Christian-born peasants captured in childhood and converted to Islam. The more promising youths, brought up in the imperial palace, became pashas, provincial governors and even grand viziers, yet they remained slaves while presiding—as the power behind the throne—over the exotic society portrayed here.

Astride horses adorned with gold and jewels, two
royal falconers display their hooded birds.
To keep the Sultan's secrets, the tongues of such
slaves were cut out to render them mute.

Soldiers of the Sultan's bodyguard, chosen from the elite 12,000-man corps of Janizaries, parade with spectacular headdresses, including a fortress that can shoot live fireworks.

Dispensing the Sultan's largesse, the Ottoman minister of finance throws silver to the crowd while two bareheaded slaves wrestle over some coins that have fallen to the ground.

A squad of heavily armed Janizaries wearing
elaborate headdresses of horsetails—the
Ottoman emblem of rank and power—escort a
model of a Turkish war galley on parade.

The military was preeminent in Turkish society for a good reason: Unlike the mercantile nations of Europe, the Ottoman Empire depended on constant warfare for its survival.

The imperial treasury was financed primarily by the spoils of war—taxes levied on conquered states and the Sultan's one-fifth share of captured booty. The slave ranks of the government bureaucracy could be replenished only by new captives. And the leaders of the *sipahis*, freebooting feudal warriors who composed the bulk of the Turkish army, had the most powerful incentive of all: They were not paid in cash but with fiefs in the territories they conquered.

Groups of picked marksmen like these, who were expert with both firearms and bow, were employed as reinforcements for the soldiery aboard each Turkish war galley.

Accompanied by a Panpipe, a street-corner band of navy recruiters sing of glory and adventure in order to entice paupers onto the rowing benches of their war galleys.

Ascetic, bare-chested dervishes pierce their
skin with knives, arrows, swords, maces
and even a lance to prove their devotion to Islam
—and to garner alms from spectators.

As proof of the supposed barbarity and fanaticism of the Muslim faith, most Christians focused on such grisly aspects of Turkish society as those below. However, thoughtful observers admitted that Islamic zeal, despite its sometimes bizarre manifestations, imbued the subjects of the omnipotent Sultan with extraordinary devotion and discipline, both in battle and in civilian life.

"They are very pious adherents of their false religion," one Venetian ambassador conceded. "It would be more difficult to govern 2,000 Christians than 100,000 Turks—and much more difficult if the Christians were Italians!"

Supervised by officials of the court, the Sultan's executioners hoist hog-tied convicts up the gallows, then impale them on immense iron hooks—an execution reserved for traitors.

A professional muscleman, wrapped tightly in chains, allows members of his troupe to stone him in order to honor the Sultan and show off his own prodigious strength.

Fight to the finish at Lepanto

Galleys of the Ottoman Empire, the Muslim rival of Christian Europe, collide with those of Venice and its allies in a decisive battle at Lepanto in 1571.

arly in September of 1571 a papal nuncio arrived at the great Sicilian port of Messina, bringing Pope Pius V's prophecy of a Holy League victory over the heathen Ottomans. For the union of Venice, Spain and the papacy had not died. Despite the military setbacks of the previous year and a series of diplomatic setbacks during the spring of 1571, their unofficial treaty had finally been confirmed, and now the harbor of Messina glittered with a swaying forest of masts.

This was surely the most powerful fleet ever launched by Christendom; it was almost entirely composed of heavily armed war galleys. All through the century the importance of artillery had grown, and nearly every galley in this armada boasted at least three cannon mounted low on the deck and peering menacingly over the bow. Most awesome of all were the galleasses—a refitted version of the Venetian great galley. Measuring 160 feet in length and 40 feet in beam, they were powered by some 50 oars (with as many as six men to an oar) and carried a battery of about 30 guns on platforms at bow and stern.

Among the fleet's 213-sail fighting force, the ships of Venice were preponderant, numbering 105 war galleys and six galleasses. Eighty-one additional galleys—more powerfully armed though slower and less maneuverable than those of the Venetian design—were gathered under the aegis of Spain (including contingents from her dominions of Naples and Sicily). The Pope sent a flotilla of 12 galleys, and Genoa, Savoy and the Knights of Saint John contributed three each. Some 50 lightly armed, swift and maneuverable *fragatas*—small relatives of the galley—were on hand as messengers. The only oarless ships in the fleet were 20 or so round ships mustered as supply carriers—for one of the lessons learned from the Battle of Zonchio three quarters of a century before was that the round ship, totally dependent on sails, lacked the maneuverability to engage swift Ottoman galleys.

According to some accounts, the fleet in Messina harbor was joined one night by another ship. Painted jet black, and even carrying black sails, she slid like a dream among the Christian vessels, noiseless and unchallenged. This was the ship of the corsair Karakoch, sent by the Ottomans to spy on the Christians. All night she glided up and down the lines of ships, counting galleys, galleasses and round ships, then departed before dawn, unnoticed.

So, already reconnoitered, the Holy League's offensive began. It was, perhaps, the last of the Crusades—for here, in a brief and heady moment, fractious Christian nations were united by a strong Pope against the Muslim power that had surged out of the East and the South. Never, in fact, had the Turk seemed so numerous.

"He is stronger than we in the numbers of his vessels," wrote the commander of the Christian fleet, Don Juan of Austria, "but not so, I believe, in quality either of vessels or of men. I trust our Lord that He will give us the victory."

The quality of Christian leaders was superior too. Don Juan himself, appointed by the Pope, was the paragon of his age. The illegitimate son of the great Charles V, Holy Roman Emperor and King of Spain, he was now a mere 24 years old, a dashing figure with long, curled hair. Arriv-

In this relief, Pope Pius V—attended by cardinals, nobles and an assortment of mythological heroes—presents his personal standard to Marc Antonio Colonna, the Roman admiral of the Holy League's papal squadron. An iron-willed leader, the Pontiff singlehandedly persuaded Spain and Venice to forgo their chronic feuding and join the papacy to combat the Ottoman menace.

ing fresh from victories over rebels in Spain, he charmed the heterogeneous soldiers under his command with his tact and manliness.

His generals included two who had failed the previous year—the courageous but inexpert papal commander, Marc Antonio Colonna, and the cautious Genoese Gian Andrea Doria, whose reluctance to fight had crippled the previous allied expedition. But with them was the impetuously daring Don Juan de Cardona, general of the Sicilian squadron, and a tried and formidable admiral, Don Alvaro de Bazán, one of the foremost naval commanders of his day, who had excelled in Spain's warfare against both the French and the Turks.

As for the Venetians, dogged by chronic lack of manpower, they had pushed themselves to the breaking point. Exiles, mercenaries, mainlanders—all were called into service as soldiers and oarsmen. "Yesterday I began to visit the galleys of the Venetians," wrote Don Juan to his secretary on August 30, "and went on board the flagship. You cannot believe what bad order both the soldiers and the sailors were in. Arms and artillery they certainly have, but as fighting is not to be done without men, a certain spasm takes me when I see with what materials I am expected by the world to do something of importance."

But among the Venetians there was no sign of those pigeonhearted captains who had failed so miserably only a year before. This time the high command went to no privileged merchant but to the Governor of Crete, Sebastiano Venier, a bad-tempered but thoroughly competent old servant of the republic. In the portraits of him that remain, this grizzled warrior—he was already 75 years old—stares out from beneath a thicket of white eyebrows with a look of suppressed fury. He had the appearance, and temper, of an aged lion. His body was reputedly covered with scars from countless brawls, and nobody knew how many tankards of beer had been broken over his head. Beneath him ranked two *provveditori* from the august patrician families of Barbarigo and Quirini, fighters as well as merchants.

One and all, the Venetian officers were anxious to fight, intent as they were on the relief of Cyprus, where the port of Famagusta, when last they heard, still held out heroically against a huge army of Turks and a supporting armada. However, the Christian fleet did not plan to make for Cyprus first, but to sail against a great Turkish armada that was ravaging Venetian possessions on the western coast of Greece.

At dawn on September 16—late in the year and risking storms—the allied fleet moved in massive array out of Messina harbor. The papal nuncio, standing on the end of the jetty surrounded by churchmen in shimmering robes, blessed each ship as it swept past him out to sea. At the head of the Spanish contingent, beneath the standard of the league, Don Juan sailed in the 70-oar war galley *Real (Royal)*, packed with more than 400 oarsmen and as many fighting men. Beside him went the galley of papal Captain General Colonna, and that of Venier beneath the standard of Saint Mark. By midmorning the Strait of Messina was filled with quivering pennants and swollen sails as the great fleet cruised toward the mainland of Italy. It anchored for the night off the Italian coast on a front five miles long.

Three days later, while the fleet sheltered from storm in the lee of Cape

Colonne, at the entrance of the Gulf of Taranto, the commanders heard disquieting news. The Turkish armada they sought was apparently dispersing to the south and east and might never confront them. But that night, above the watchful fleet, a brilliant meteor flashed across the sky, illuminating the whole sea, then exploded in a triple pathway of fire. It seemed to portend some enormous event.

Unbeknown to the Christians, that event could no longer be the relief of Cyprus—only revenge. More than a month before, Famagusta had fallen. For 10 months its handful of Venetian and Greek troops—fewer than 10,000 against a besieging army of some 250,000—had held out valiantly under an inspired commander, Marc Antonio Bragadin; but by midsummer a blistering series of attacks and counterattacks had drained their strength. From their splendid bulwarks they watched helplessly as the Turkish sappers wormed forward, creating a fantastical maze of trenches—a network so extensive, according to some accounts, that it could absorb the whole Ottoman army and so deep that only the lance tips of advancing cavalry showed above it.

At last the Turks stormed the outworks of the city's great landgate and poured in to the attack; but beneath the gate the Venetians had laid a giant mine, and with this they blew 1,000 Turks and 100 of their own men to pieces. Once again the attack faltered. Crowded behind make-shift palisades of casks and sandbags, the defenders—starved, exhausted, and wracked by disease—were reduced to eating horses, donkeys and cats. The Turks attacked again with determined fury. Their losses were terrible. But within the city at least two thirds of the garrison lay dead, and on August 1, Bragadin negotiated a truce by which—he thought—his troops and the townspeople would be spared.

The allied battle fleet and its commanders, gazing skyward as the meteor burst and faded in the night of September 19, clung to their vision of effecting a miraculous rescue. On September 24, after rounding Cape Santa Maria, the heel of Italy, they steered for Greece across the stormy mouth of the Adriatic. The Sicilian commander, Cardona, took the van with seven swift reconnaissance galleys, ranging over the sea some 20 miles in front of the rest; but toward evening he drew back to within eight miles of the main fleet. At nightfall the weather was unsettled. Each squadron moved in line ahead, its admiral and his staff staring into blackness from the lead vessel. In the rear of each line, a dissociated orb of fire moved in silence through the night where the hindmost ship dangled a lantern from the masthead.

Recent reports contradicted earlier intelligence about the Turkish fleet. It had not dispersed at all but had raided Corfu and was now making for the Gulf of Lepanto, only 150 miles ahead of the Christian force. The next morning, through a curtain of rain, the reefs and islands of northwestern Greece became dimly discernible, and there the Christian fleet sought shelter from a gathering storm. Two days later, when the skies had cleared, the fleet sailed into the harbor of the shattered island of Corfu, which had been attacked by the Turks two weeks before. Although the raiders had left Corfu's fort and its terrified garrison alone, they had gutted the villages. Christian soldiers who went ashore for food and water found every church desecrated: crucifixes broken, frescoed

In an imaginative Turkish re-creation of the 10-month siege of Famagusta—the last Venetian stronghold on Cyprus—Turkish warriors coax skittish horses off a gangplank (left) to reinforce the imperial cavalry, while another ship waits offshore (foreground) and a handful of mounted Turks watch from the hilltops.

saints slashed by scimitars and their eyes used for target practice.

For the last time the commanders of the league met in formal council. It was a meeting pregnant with history. The Turkish fleet, they had heard, had entered the Gulf of Lepanto, which had been a Turkish haven ever since the Ottomans had wrested its fortress from the Venetians in 1499. The enemy fleet reportedly numbered 300 vessels, including 160 fine galleys; but its men, apparently, were weak with fever, and its commanders were divided. In council the more circumspect spirits—Doria among them—advised against battle. If the Christian fleet suffered defeat, they argued, the whole Mediterranean would be exposed to the sword of the infidel. But the feelings of the majority prevailed. The Venetians were so belligerent that they threatened to fight alone if they were forced to, and Don Juan himself was determined to bring the Ottomans to battle.

On September 29, Venier embarked 4,000 troops from the garrison of Corfu, and for the next two days the entire fleet held musketry and gunnery exercises, and then was reviewed by Don Juan. Volleys of gunfire hailed him as he sailed by, but the harquebuses that the men fired with such enthusiasm produced several casualties. Since the fleet's assembly at Messina, wrote an officer, some 20 men had been killed this way; it was now decreed that any soldier who shot off ball as well as powder in such celebrations would be sentenced to death.

While the fleet still lingered off Corfu, the whole enterprise was jeopardized by an outbreak of internecine violence. Many of the Venetian galleys, badly undermanned, had been obliged to take on board Spanish infantrymen, and on one of these vessels, the *Armed Man*, a furious riot broke out. According to eyewitness accounts, a Spanish soldier, disturbed from his sleep, began bickering with a Venetian sailor, and the quarrel spread. The Spanish musketeers laid about them with the fork rests of their guns, the Venetian sailors and oarsmen snatched out knives, and soon the deck was littered with dead and wounded. The leader of the Spaniards was a fiery Tuscan named Muzio. Far from quieting his men, he told the Venetian galley captain to go to the devil, drew his sword and joined in the fight.

The captain quickly sent word to Venier's flagship. "Sir," the messenger announced, "the Spanish contingent in the *Armed Man* have risen and are killing the crew." Venier, furious, dispatched his provost marshal with four men to arrest the mutineers, but when they approached the ship they were met by Muzio, armed with a harquebus. Two of the emissaries were tossed into the sea, while Muzio shot the provost marshal through the chest.

Venier fell into an awesome rage. He ordered that the *Armed Man* be forcibly boarded, and when the Spaniards threatened to open fire, he prepared to cannonade the vessel as if she were a hostile galley. At this moment a Spanish ship intervened, carrying a senior officer from Muzio's corps, who shouted to Venier from the poop: "Your Excellency, leave it to me. I am on my way to the *Armed Man*, and I will return these men to obedience."

Venier believed that if he allowed a Spaniard to interfere in the discipline on Venetian ships, his authority would be eroded, and he was determined to keep matters in his own hands. "By the blood of Christ," the crusty veteran bellowed back to the Spaniard, "take no action, unless you wish me to sink your galley and all your soldiers. I will bring these dogs to heel without your assistance."

And so he did. A party of Venetian harquebusiers swarmed over the *Armed Man* and seized the leading mutineers. Venier was still in a rage when Muzio was brought before him.

"Hang him!" Venier shouted, jerking his thumb toward the yardarm. And it was done. "Any more culprits?"

A Spanish corporal and two soldiers were pushed forward.

"Hang them too!" Venier roared.

Muzio's Spanish superior officer, meanwhile, had returned to Don Juan to report how Venier had prevented him from boarding the *Armed Man*. As they were talking on the flagship, one of Don Juan's staff exclaimed, "Look, sir," and pointed. Clearly visible, swinging from the yardarm of Venier's galley, were four bodies.

"What is that?" burst out Don Juan. "Who has dared to authorize executions without my permission? Has the general of the republic of Saint Mark had the audacity to commit so grave an affront to my authority? Has he received any such power from the King of Spain and His Holiness? By God I will no longer tolerate the arrogance of this old fool that Venice has placed in command of her galleys!"

Some of his officers at once talked of opening fire on the Venetian ships, and it took Bazán, Colonna and Barbarigo—all afraid for the fleet's unity—to calm Don Juan down. "All right," he said at last. "I will do my duty. I will forgive Venier, but I do not wish to see him again." Then he ordered: "To your ships, gentlemen, and we will put to sea."

The Turks too had been in council at their fortress of Lepanto. By chance, what they said has survived—reported by Venetian prisoners who were present and were later ransomed. The council majority, it seems, was in favor of sailing out to fight, but some of its most prestigious members were not. The enemy fleet, they said, was superior to any put to sea by Christian nations before; it was better not to seek an engagement, but to lie under the shore batteries of Lepanto and wait. However, the supreme Ottoman commander, Müezzinzade Ali Pasha, was a courageous and experienced leader who had sailed from the Turkish base at Negroponte with orders to seek out the Christian fleet. His men were fired by their recent success in sacking coastal towns, and his confederate, the Algerian corsair Uluch Ali, flatly declared that they would all be branded as cowards if they stayed at Lepanto "looking after the women and children." Soon afterward, orders arrived from the capital that left Ali Pasha no alternative. Sultan Selim II had heard of Famagusta's fall. Drunk with success as well as wine, he ordered his commander to capture the Christian fleet and tow it to Constantinople at once.

Late September found the Turkish armada revictualing at Lepanto. Sick men were replaced, and the soldiers replenished by fresh Janizaries, *sipahis*—these were dismounted cavalry—and irregulars. In all, the Muslim troops on board numbered some 88,000. Their war fleet of 274 galleys and galiots was even bigger than that of the Christians, and its

commanders were hardened and brave. Besides Ali Pasha himself they included Mehmed Suluk, Governor of Alexandria, and—above all— Uluch Ali, the most feared seaman of his age.

Like many of the corsairs, Uluch Ali was Christian by birth—a native of Calabria in southern Italy. Captured by Barbary corsairs, he eventually renounced Christianity for Islam and joined his captors. His talent and ruthlessness procured him successively the captaincy of a ship, the rank of Pasha of Algiers and the viceroyalty of Algiers under the Ottoman Empire. Now a wind-tanned warrior in his seventies, he led into battle an agile squadron of 93 Algerian galleys and galiots.

But Uluch Ali, along with the other Ottoman commanders, underestimated the strength of the Christians. Karakoch, the intrepid corsair who had reconnoitered the allied fleet at Messina harbor, had apparently done his counting before the Christian armada was at full strength; he had returned with an estimate that was 50 galleys short of the reality. The reports of Greek fishermen also belittled the Christian numbers— either because the entire fleet was rarely in view at one time, or because the fishermen wanted to please the Turks. So, on the night of October 6, full of confidence, the Ottoman fleet set sail westward from Lepanto, in search of battle.

The Christians also had underestimated the enemy's strength. A week before, they had received reports that the Ottoman fleet numbered 300 galleys and that 60 had been detached for the transport and replacement of the sick. On the evening of October 5 a Turkish renegade—probably a double agent—reported that the Ottoman strength had been further reduced to 100 galleys and that plague was raging among its men. By now the Christians were anxious only that the Turks did not evade them and that they catch the imperial fleet of Ali Pasha and the Algerian squadron of Uluch Ali together.

That same evening brought news that enraged the Venetians—the report of Famagusta's fall and of the death of its commander, Marc Antonio Bragadin, who had agreed to an honorable truce. The Turkish commander, going back on his word, had taken prisoner the pitiful remnant of the Venetian garrison. He had lopped off Bragadin's nose and ears and then forced the mutilated Venetian leader to haul stone and earth for work on the fortress. Bragadin was then flayed alive in front of Famagusta's desecrated cathedral. And even this, it seemed, did not satisfy the victors, for Bragadin's skin was stuffed with straw, placed astride a cow and paraded beneath a scarlet parasol through the streets of the captured city.

In a mood of black fury, the men of the allied fleet weighed anchor at 2 o'clock on the morning of Sunday, October 7, and approached the Gulf of Lepanto along the ragged shoals and islets of western Greece. The sea was choppy, and a southeast wind blew in their faces. As dawn broke and the allied vanguard advanced into the mouth of the gulf, Don Juan issued orders that Mass be said throughout the fleet. Almost simultaneously, his watchmen in the ship's maintop sighted two sail in the distance. Soon they reported four sail, then eight. And within a few minutes the whole Turkish armada had risen over the horizon and was bearing toward them.

It was an anxious moment for Don Juan; his fleet was stretched out for miles along the coast behind him. At once he sent out *fragatas* to urge the stragglers on—"letting fall some holy curses," added one chronicler—and began to form his battle line across the mouth of the gulf.

The Turks too had been straining their eyes to catch sight of the enemy fleet. But at first they saw only the Sicilian vanguard of Cardona, with a few advance galleys; the rest of the Christian ships were hidden from view by a rocky headland to the north. For a while the Muslims thought that they had found an easy prey, but slowly more and more of the allied ships broke clear of land and began thickening over the sea. Impatiently the Ottoman officers demanded reports from their watchmen in the topsails, and always the replies came back of new additions to the Christian strength. Soon the officers were cursing Karakoch for his misleading intelligence, and their mood turned from jubilation to a grim fierceness.

The Christian ships, meanwhile, began maneuvering into line abreast with purposeful discipline, each warship so close to its neighbor that no

Fragile alliance against the heathen

For sheer combustibility, few alliances in history rival the Holy League of Venice, Spain and the papacy. The negotiations, held in late 1570 and early 1571, often seemed a litany of totally irreconcilable aims. Venice wanted to save Cyprus from the Turks, Spain wanted to fight the Turks only on the Barbary Coast, and Pope Pius V envisioned a crusade against the infidels wherever they were found.

Spain, mistrusting Venice, insisted on automatic excommunication of any state that withdrew from the league. The Pope rejected the proposal, but Spain had good reason to be suspicious: It later turned out that Venice had stalled the talks for months while secretly—and unsuccessfully—negotiating with the Turks.

After the treaty was signed, the fractious allied commanders (right) were held together by their leader, Don Juan of Austria, long enough to confront the Turks at the Battle of Lepanto in October 1571. But the flimsy pact collapsed within three years.

Gian Andrea Doria, a Genoese admiral, went to Lepanto with special commendation from Spain's King Philip II, who urged Don Juan to take no action without consulting Doria.

Don Juan of Austria (above) was repeatedly accused of favoring one or another of the allies. He once wrote to the Doge: "My ill-wishers, weary of making me out to be so great a Venetian, now say I neglect Your Serenity."

Agostino Barbarigo, the Venetian
second-in-command, was quiet in council
but utterly courageous in battle. When
his fellow commanders at Lepanto heard
he was mortally wounded, they fought
with redoubled fury to avenge him.

Spain's Don Alvaro de Bazán
(below) was the Holy League's
most respected admiral.
Gian Andrea Doria, who at first
disagreed with the Lepanto
battle plan, assented only
after Bazán gave his approval.

Although Marc Antonio Colonna
(above), Grand Constable of Spanish
Naples, was a soldier and not a
sailor, he was named second-in-
command of the fleet by Pius V
in order to win Spain to the alliance.

Sebastiano Venier, the impetuous
Venetian commander, hated Genoese
leader Gian Andrea Doria. On
learning that Doria was to inspect the
Venetian contingent, Venier
threatened to kill any Genoese who
dared approach his ship.

enemy could row between. It was vital that the Holy League fleet, with its huge weight of prow-mounted cannon, should maintain a solid line-abreast formation and meet the Muslims head on. The Muslim galleys, though less powerful, were quicker and more maneuverable than their Christian opponents; their chief hope of victory lay in precipitating a general melee and then attacking Christian galleys from the sides and rear, where they were only lightly gunned.

Following a plan devised at Messina, the Holy League fleet resolved itself into four great squadrons—right, left, center and reserve (maps, pages 147-149). Venetians, Spanish, Genoese and papal ships were mingled side by side in each squadron to prevent any panicking allied commander from withdrawing his entire contingent in midbattle. In the center squadron of 64 galleys sailed Don Juan himself in the *Real,* with Venier in the Venetian flagship on one side and the papal commander, Colonna, on the other. Also in this squadron was the small but redoubtable flotilla of the Knights of Saint John. The whole center group flew blue pennants from its mastheads.

The left wing, under the Venetian *provveditore* Agostino Barbarigo, comprised 53 galleys, 41 of them Venetian and all flying yellow banderoles at their foreyards. In this squadron went some of the republic's proudest war galleys: the *Fortune,* the *Sea Horse,* the *Christ Raised* and the *Great Christ Risen Again.* It was no accident that Venetian ships predominated in this group, which was charged with protecting the inshore flank of the Christian fleet. Here the Muslim galleys stood their best chance of outflanking the Holy League fleet, since their shallow drafts allowed them to maneuver close to land. Of the Christian ships the Venetian galleys were the lightest and quickest; they alone could counter the threat.

The right wing, under the command of Doria, numbered 54 vessels, flying green pennants. But these galleys, occupying the southernmost station, had the farthest to go before they reached their positions and were still maneuvering even when the battle began. In the rear of the fleet, with a reserve of 38, showing white pennants astern, came the Spaniard Don Alvaro de Bazán, who was ordered to bolster any part of the line that wavered or was in serious danger.

As the Turkish sails grew distinct in the clear Greek light, the six Venetian galleasses, impregnably high and bristling with guns but too heavy to maneuver quickly, were towed by galleys toward a position 1,000 yards in front of the battle line, where—like floating bastions—they could break up the enemy advance with their artillery. The galleasses on the left wing were commanded by relatives of the dead and defiled commander Bragadin, who were hot for revenge. These, and the two galleasses in the center, reached their positions before the battle began, but the two on the right could not be towed into place in time.

Now the Turkish armada—divided into four squadrons like the Holy League fleet—was approaching up the gulf with a light wind behind. It advanced in a huge crescent formation, presenting a concave front to the Christians, one edge of its battle line running through the shallows of the northern coast, the other reaching out toward the Peloponnesian shore to the south. Don Juan, clothed in full armor, left the *Real* for a swift

Circuitous routes to the showdown

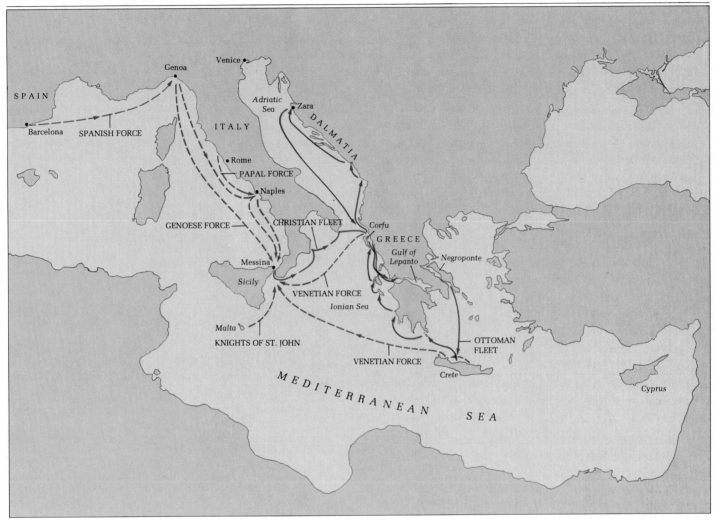

While the far-flung forces of the Holy League (dashed red lines) assembled at Messina before confronting the Ottoman fleet, the Turks (green line) attacked Crete, sacked Venetian outposts in Greece and Dalmatia, and sent a squadron as far north as Zara in search of enemy ships. Then they withdrew into the Gulf of Lepanto, where the combined Christian fleet (solid red line) found them on October 7, 1571.

fragata and sailed across the front of much of the Christian line, holding up a crucifix. To the Spaniards he cried out: "My children, we are here to conquer or to die as heaven may determine. Do not let our impious foe ask us, 'Where is your God?' " To the Venetians, harrowed by the loss of Cyprus and the sacking of many outposts, he appealed for revenge on the Turks. As he passed Venier's flagship, he was wise enough to say a few courteous words to the old lion. Venier, standing on his poop in full armor, answered genially back, and they parted friends.

So began the last great battle ever to be fought between galleys. The Christians were well prepared. They had cut off their galleys' sharp prows (normally used as boarding bridges in flank attacks), so that the forward guns—cast-bronze muzzle-loading cannon with an effective range of some 500 yards—could strike the bows of the enemy in a hard and low trajectory. Some of the ships had been heightened fore and aft by bulwarks of shields, canvas and cordage. In the Holy League fleet, Christian convicts at the oars were released from their chains, given arms and promised their freedom if they fought; at the same time the manacles of Muslim galley slaves aboard the Christian ships were reinforced by extra handcuffs that restricted their reach to the pulling of the oars.

Each fleet, as it approached the other, was awed by the enemy's numbers. Beyond the isolated Venetian galleasses the Turks could make out a huge legion of 209 galleys in which gleamed the massed armor of awakened Christendom, while the Christians, staring ahead, saw an armada of 274 galleys and galiots and a cloud of smaller vessels. In the Turkish center, which numbered 125 galleys and galiots, moved Ali Pasha in his flagship *Sultana*, surrounded by the flagships of his commanders and governors. In the right wing, facing Barbarigo and the Christian left, sailed the Governor of Alexandria, Mehmed Suluk, with 54 galleys and two galiots, including a strong contingent of his own Alexandrian galleys. And on the Turkish left, intent on outflanking the Holy League's right wing, were the 93 galleys and swift Algerian galiots of Uluch Ali. Of the 88,000 fighting men on board the Turkish fleet, some 5,000 belonged to the dreaded corps of Janizaries, and many of the sailors and captains were long skilled in the ways of the sea.

Seeing the strength of the Christian fleet, Ali Pasha retracted the arms of his crescent to form a long, straight line. He watched the enemy now with profound unease. The presence of the galleasses worried him, and the number of Spanish galleys—so strong in men and artillery—filled him with apprehension. Ali Pasha, an intelligent and sensitive man, had always shown toward his Christian galley slaves a humanity rare for the era, and he now walked between their benches and addressed them in Spanish: "Friends, I expect you today to carry out your duty to me in return for the good treatment you have received. I promise you your liberty if I win the battle; if the day is yours, God has given it to you."

Suddenly, from the galley beside his, a cry went up that the Christian right wing, under Doria, had broken its order and was fleeing. At once a Genoese renegade, who might be expected to understand his fellow countryman's maneuvers, was sent aloft to report. Seeing the sails of the squadron shifting and spreading southward, this man realized that Doria was merely extending his line to avoid being outflanked by Uluch Ali. He came down the rigging shaking his head. "Doria is not flying," he said. "God grant it may not turn out the other way."

The allied line now extended some four miles across the gulf, and the more seasoned Ottoman commanders were taking alarm. Uluch Ali is said to have urged Ali Pasha to fall back on the shore batteries of Lepanto, but the admiral replied: "I will never give the impression that my fleet is in retreat before the Christians. We are definitely going to fight."

Soon afterward the more cautious Christian commanders, while receiving their last orders on the *Real*, were likewise trying to dissuade Don Juan from fighting. Chilled by the sight of the vast Ottoman armada, they reminded him that the Turks, if defeated, could retreat to Lepanto, whereas the Christian fleet would face annihilation. "Gentlemen," replied Don Juan, dismissing them, "the time for counsel is past, and the time for fighting has come."

It was 11 o'clock. The wind that had blown behind the Turks since dawn suddenly dropped, and the sea smoothed to a glassy lake. In unison the galleys of the Ottoman fleet dropped their sails and lowered their yards and masts. The movement was so concerted and precise that the Christians were struck with admiration. But at the same time they took heart, for it seemed to them that the wind's failure—it was no longer helping the enemy—was a sign from God.

As the two fleets drew closer together, a hush spread over them. The Muslims quietly prayed. Meanwhile, at the center of the Christian line, Don Juan fell on his knees, imploring God's blessing on the enterprise. His action was copied by every man in the fleet whose hands were not occupied with pulling an oar. Spanish and papal harquebusiers, Genoese seamen, Maltese knights, Venetian swordsmen, Neapolitan marines, Sicilian pikemen—all knelt in unison on the decks beside their weapons. The only sounds were those of creaking oars and the lisping of the water at the prows. Gunners, with wicks already lighted in their hands, prayed beside their cannon; musketeers knelt with their firearms couched over the bulwarks. In all that multitude, only the friars and monks stood upright in the ships' prows, lifting crucifixes to the sky. Franciscans, Dominicans and Jesuits, they sprinkled holy water on the bowed heads, pronouncing indulgence to those who fought and absolution to those who were to fall.

While still several miles away, Ali Pasha's flagship, the *Sultana*, fired a gun in salute. A gun from Don Juan's *Real* answered him. A second Turkish shot cracked out; a second Christian cannon answered; then the two flagships set a course for each other.

It was later said that at this hour, in the quietness of the Vatican in Rome, the Pope was talking to his financial advisers. Suddenly he stopped, went to open a window and for a long time stared into the sky. Then he turned to his treasurer and said: "This is no time for business. Go and give thanks to God, for our fleet is about to meet the Turks, and God will give us the victory." Peering back into the room a moment later, the treasurer saw the old man on his knees before a crucifix, with his hands lifted in prayer.

The Christian soldiers rose to their feet again. Trumpets sounded and bands played. And Don Juan, wrote an officer of the fleet, "was so eager for the fray that in youthful high spirits, with two cavaliers, he danced a graceful hornpipe on the fighting platform of his galley."

Now the oars of the Turkish armada dipped and lashed furiously into the sea. The fleet's rank and file, ignorant of their commanders' misgivings, yelled to the Christians to come on and be massacred "like drowned hens." They danced and stamped to cymbals, tambours, clappers and flutes; clashed their swords and spears; and fired musket volleys into the air.

Then, minutes after noon, the Turks opened fire. A shot clipped the pennant of Cardona's vessel. The guns of one of the Venetian galleasses promptly opened up on Ali Pasha's flagship. The first shot crashed through the ceremonial triple lantern in the *Sultana's* stern—an evil portent. "God grant," murmured the Pasha from the quarter-deck, "we may be able to give a good answer to this question." The next shot splintered the poop of a galley alongside his, and soon the galleasses' fire was hitting the Turks in a steady blizzard, ripping through several galleys and sinking two of them outright, so that Ali Pasha ordered his fleet not to attack those terrible floating castles but to pass them by as quickly as possible.

"Their smoke and thunder engulfed the enemy," a Venetian historian proudly wrote, "and balls, chains and grapeshot were flung from them with incredible fury, smashing a great part of the armada, decapitating this man, cutting that one in two, breaking masts in pieces, cracking the forecastles of some and the poops of others, or sweeping away whole banks of oars, and finally hurling some to the bottom, with the loss of many drowned." The Turkish fleet was thrown out of order; the Ottoman galleys jostled one behind the next, obstructing one another's fire, while the galleasses' guns flashed and thundered. When the main fleets met, the cannon in the bows of the Christian galleys raked the Ottoman attackers with a second cruel fire; but the Turkish ships came on in confused clusters, their crews rowing through the smoke and loosing a tempest of shot and arrows, trying to find gaps in the Christian line in order to attack it from behind.

The Ottoman right wing, under Mehmed Suluk, moving against Barbarigo's squadron on the Christian left, was hit by a crippling fire from the galleasses of Bragadin's kinsmen. But the shallow-draft Muslim vessels persevered in their course, rowing hard to cut inshore and turn the Christian flank.

"Our left wing," wrote Girolamo Diedo, a Venetian officer, "was assailed by a line already broken and by vessels in disorder. But Mehmed Suluk and Kara Ali"—a redoubtable corsair—"outpacing all the other Ottoman galleys, drove furiously toward our line. As they neared the Aetolian shore, they slid between the shallows with the foremost ships of their squadron. These waterways were familiar to them; they knew exactly the depth of the sea above the shoals. Followed by four or five galleys, they planned to take our left wing in the rear."

But Barbarigo, himself sailing on the extreme left flank of the Christian division, turned his galley about and attacked the enemy in the shallows. He was followed by other Venetian and Neapolitan vessels; more Ottoman ships crowded to the struggle, and soon a bitter fight was raging among the reefs.

Despite Barbarigo's vigilance, several Turkish vessels bypassed him and fell on the rear of his squadron. His own galley was surrounded by five of the enemy, Mehmed Suluk's among them, and fought alone for nearly an hour, enveloped in a storm of arrows. He directed his men with inspired courage and expertise while the shafts rained around him. Soon the ceremonial lantern behind him bristled with Turkish arrows. A boarding party of Janizaries swept half his ship clear, then was hurled back by a counterattack. So that his commands could be heard more clearly, Barbarigo raised the visor of his helmet. Almost immediately an arrow struck him in the left eye, and he was carried below, mortally wounded. His nephew, Giovanni Marino Contarini, came alongside in his own galley and cleared the rest of Barbarigo's ship of Janizaries, but he too was killed.

Then the tide turned. The terrible fire of the harquebusiers decimated the Ottoman soldiers as they massed along the ships' decks, whereas the barricaded bows of the Christian vessels helped protect against Turkish

Bold variations on textbook tactics

Galley fleets traditionally fought in a tight line-abreast formation—for a good reason. Though galleys carried a formidable battery of bow-mounted cannon, their undefended sides were fatally vulnerable to flank attack. In a closely knit line, each galley shielded her neighbors' sides; if the line was too loose it could be shattered by opponents darting between galleys.

Maintaining tight formations for a large battle such as Lepanto required great discipline, because a line of galleys nearly two miles long tended to behave like a string of children playing crack-the-whip: When one vessel momentarily lagged behind or surged ahead, its neighbors slowly did the same one after another, magnifying the error and often opening huge gaps between galleys.

This problem rendered fleet maneuvers virtually impossible, so the standard tactics of galley warfare were simple. The two battle lines slowly rowed toward each other until they were about 500 yards apart, then burst forward and crashed together for a one-on-one slug fest.

Fleets generally were organized like land armies, with a center division and two flank divisions. Because extremely long lines tended to fall apart, the center division usually comprised no more than 65 galleys, and the flank divisions, which needed greater mobility, slightly fewer.

The fleets that met at Lepanto on October 7, 1571, were organized in classical formations, but both planned variations on the conventional tactics. The Christians, hoping to shatter the Ottoman formation at one stroke, ordered their big galleasses out ahead of the main line and concentrated their heavily gunned lantern galleys in the center. The Turks, fearing that their light galleys would be mauled in a head-on confrontation, planned to outflank the Christian right and left, then fall on the enemy from the rear.

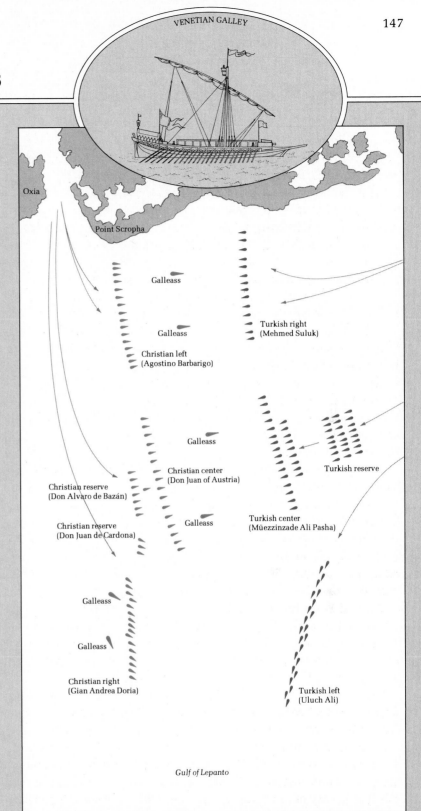

At about 11 a.m. the opposing fleets began to close for battle. The Christian right wing, however, having the farthest to row after emerging from the strait between Oxia and the mainland, had not reached its assigned position. To exploit the resulting gap, the Ottoman left immediately headed southwest in a flanking maneuver. The other Turks deployed in good order, holding in reserve nearly 100 vessels. Galleys—such as the Venetian one pictured at top—are represented here by roughly one marker for every four ships, galleasses by one marker for each ship.

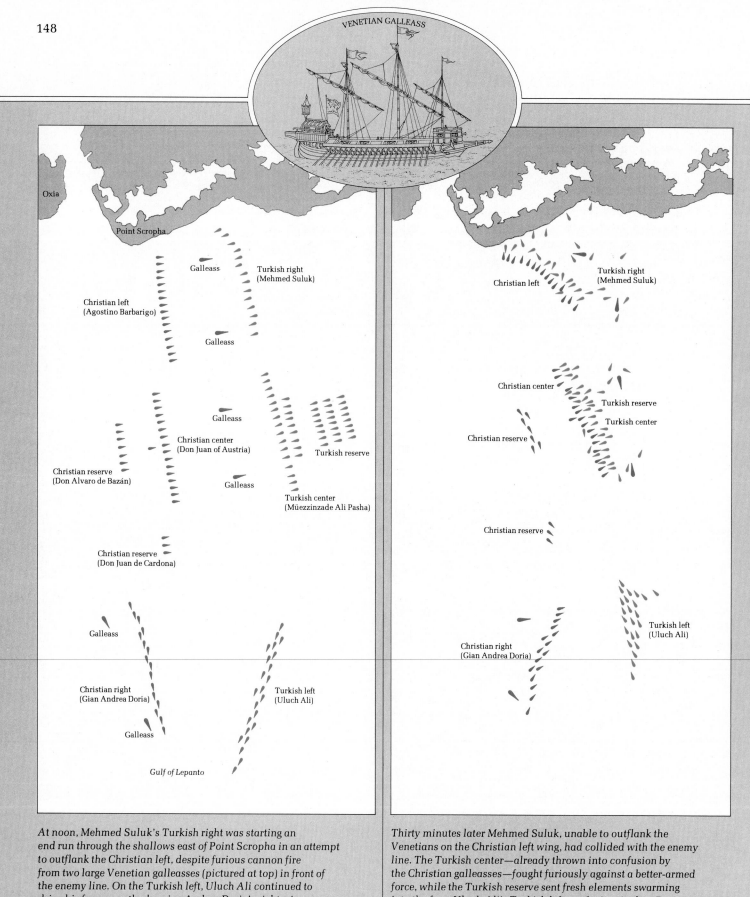

VENETIAN GALLEASS

Oxia

Point Scropha

Galleass

Turkish right
(Mehmed Suluk)

Christian left
(Agostino Barbarigo)

Galleass

Galleass

Christian center
(Don Juan of Austria)

Turkish reserve

Christian reserve
(Don Alvaro de Bazán)

Galleass

Christian reserve
(Don Juan de Cardona)

Turkish center
(Müezzinzade Ali Pasha)

Galleass

Christian right
(Gian Andrea Doria)

Turkish left
(Uluch Ali)

Galleass

Gulf of Lepanto

Christian left

Turkish right
(Mehmed Suluk)

Christian center

Turkish reserve

Turkish center

Christian reserve

Christian reserve

Turkish left
(Uluch Ali)

Christian right
(Gian Andrea Doria)

At noon, Mehmed Suluk's Turkish right was starting an
end run through the shallows east of Point Scropha in an attempt
to outflank the Christian left, despite furious cannon fire
from two large Venetian galleasses (pictured at top) in front of
the enemy line. On the Turkish left, Uluch Ali continued to
drive his forces south, drawing Andrea Doria's right wing away
from the Holy League center. To forestall a breakthrough in
the center, the galleys of the Christian reserve commanded by
Don Juan de Cardona moved into the gap left by Doria.

Thirty minutes later Mehmed Suluk, unable to outflank the
Venetians on the Christian left wing, had collided with the enemy
line. The Turkish center—already thrown into confusion by
the Christian galleasses—fought furiously against a better-armed
force, while the Turkish reserve sent fresh elements swarming
into the fray. Uluch Ali's Turkish left, outfoxing Andrea Doria,
reversed course and drove for the gap between Doria and the
Christian center; the Christian reserve turned south to intercept
this threat and Doria belatedly hurried north to catch up.

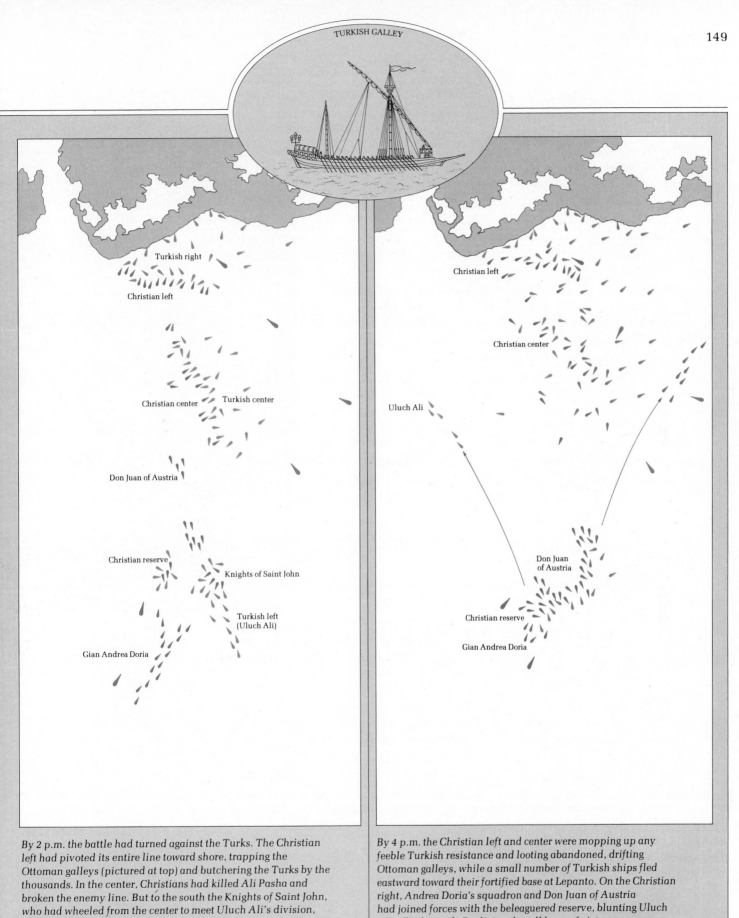

TURKISH GALLEY

Turkish right

Christian left

Christian center   Turkish center

Don Juan of Austria

Christian reserve

Knights of Saint John

Turkish left
(Uluch Ali)

Gian Andrea Doria

Christian left

Christian center

Uluch Ali

Don Juan
of Austria

Christian reserve

Gian Andrea Doria

By 2 p.m. the battle had turned against the Turks. The Christian left had pivoted its entire line toward shore, trapping the Ottoman galleys (pictured at top) and butchering the Turks by the thousands. In the center, Christians had killed Ali Pasha and broken the enemy line. But to the south the Knights of Saint John, who had wheeled from the center to meet Uluch Ali's division, had been virtually annihilated, and the Christian reserve of Don Alvaro de Bazán was hotly engaged. To protect his vulnerable rear, Don Juan of Austria rushed south to confront Uluch Ali.

By 4 p.m. the Christian left and center were mopping up any feeble Turkish resistance and looting abandoned, drifting Ottoman galleys, while a small number of Turkish ships fled eastward toward their fortified base at Lepanto. On the Christian right, Andrea Doria's squadron and Don Juan of Austria had joined forces with the beleaguered reserve, blunting Uluch Ali's flank attack. Realizing that all hope of victory was now lost, Uluch Ali led a few galleys in an escape to the northwest, while a larger Turkish contingent retreated toward Lepanto.

arrows. Soon the Venetians were sweeping over the few galleys that had outflanked them; Kara Ali was taken prisoner, and the battle spread to Mehmed Suluk's flagship. Volleys of musketry riddled the ranks of her defenders, then a rush of pikemen and swordsmen hacked the remaining Turks down or flung them overboard. Holed by cannon fire, the vessel began to sink. Mehmed Suluk was fished out of the sea by the Venetians. His wounds were so frightful that when the Venetians beheaded him minutes later it seemed an act of pity.

By this time the whole shattered right squadron of the Ottoman fleet was twisted landward, where it had followed its fallen leader. "In this vast confusion," wrote the Venetian Diedo, "many of our galleys, especially those nearest the center of the fleet, had not found opponents, so they made a general turning movement toward the left in good order and came to envelop the Turkish ships, which were still putting up a desperate resistance to ours. By this adroit maneuver they held them enclosed, as in a harbor."

Ambrosio Bragadin's galleass, turning slowly about, came at the trapped Turks too, her cannons booming. The Ottoman galleys were driven onto the shoals or beaches. They crashed into one another in a mass of tangled oars and panicking men. The Venetians pursued them mercilessly. Many of the Ottomans drowned. Others, scrambling over burning or sinking decks and floundering through the shallows, were picked off by marksmen. The Venetians hounded them onto the land, killing them among the rocks. One soldier who had lost all his weapons pinned a Turk to the ground with a sharp stick through his mouth.

"The massacre was appalling," wrote Diedo. "The right wing of the Ottomans had simply ceased to exist."

This engagement was the first to begin and end. It proved, wrote Colonna afterward, that "the Venetians are made of the same stuff as in the olden times."

Meanwhile, the Turkish and Christian centers were drawing together in a pall of smoke and fire. The flagships of Don Juan and Ali Pasha had maintained their courses for each other. From Don Juan's masthead flew the azure standard of the Holy League, blazoned with the image of Christ crucified. From Ali Pasha's fluttered a banner of white embroidery from Mecca, inscribed in gold with crossed scimitars and verses of the Koran. Upon these two great ships, it seemed to witnesses, the fate of the whole battle depended, and each was prepared for a prolonged and mortal struggle.

The *Sultana's* decks were brilliant with the plumes of 300 Janizary harquebusiers and 100 archers. Beside her rowed the galleys of the Ottoman commander of land troops, Pertev Pasha, and the Pasha of Mytilene, while behind her clustered 12 more galleys and galiots, ready to send reinforcements swarming up her sides. Don Juan, too, was supported powerfully by galleys from the rear and was hugged on either side by the flagships of Venier and Colonna. Four hundred picked harquebusiers crammed the *Real's* stockaded decks, and the whole galley was ordered like a battlefield, her different sections commanded by young knights of Don Juan's choice.

Ali Pasha's first cannon shot ripped through the *Real's* forecastle and

Miguel de Cervantes, author of the classic Don Quixote, *fought at Lepanto as a 24-year-old Spanish soldier and received a harquebus wound that maimed his left hand for life. He later marveled at the selfless valor of the Christian soldiers: "Scarcely had one fallen, never to rise again, when another takes his place; and if he too falls into the sea, another and yet another succeed him with no time at all between their deaths."*

landed among the oarsmen, spattering blood. Then the huge prow of the *Sultana* loomed menacingly through the smoke and came crashing into the *Real's* bows, penetrating as deep as the fourth rower's bench. The two ships recoiled, then drifted side by side with a splintering of oars, locked together.

There now began a bloody conflict that lasted nearly two hours. On one side the plumed and booted Janizaries (the various colors of their boots indicated rank) were poised on their flagship in awesome array, their horsetail standards jostling above them, their kettledrums pounding. On the other side gleamed the massed helmets and breastplates of the Spaniards, while their Christian oarsmen snatched up swords and pikes in their support. Don Juan, standing beneath the banner of the league, was such a conspicuous target that he was begged to go below until the first cannonade was over, but he refused. The harquebusiers fired into one another's faces at a range of only a few feet, blasting away whole ranks. The detachment on the *Real's* prow was quickly half annihilated by shot. A Spanish knight who rushed up his contingent in support was hit on the helmet by a ball that failed to pierce it, but twisted it round and knocked him unconscious, so that he died, wrote a mystified chronicler, "although he showed no sign of a wound."

Twice the Spaniards rushed the *Sultana* with pikes and swords, beating back the Turks to the mainmast. But supporting Ottoman galleys poured in fresh Janizaries. Ali Pasha himself led them in their attack, and is said to have fired many arrows with his own hand—surely the last commander to draw a bowstring in European warfare. The Christian ship's deck and masts now bristled with Turkish shafts. Two arrows struck the royal standard just beneath its crowning crucifix—a dangerous omen to the Christians. But "presently," recorded a Spanish historian, "a little monkey that was on His Highness' flagship plucked them out, broke them in its teeth and threw them into the sea."

Meanwhile, beside the *Real*, Venier's ship was locked in combat with the galley of the Ottoman army commander. Now the ferocious old Venetian came into his own. The confusion was so great that orders became useless. So he stood at his prow, firing into the Turkish ranks with a blunderbuss, which a servant beside him kept reloading with half a dozen balls at a time. "A soldier all white-haired and at the extreme of old age," wrote a contemporary historian, "Venier performed the feats of arms of a young man—like a serpent that issues out of the dark in spring, casting off his old skin for a resplendent new one, stronger than ever, his eyes flashing fire."

When his own ship was boarded, Venier led a counterattack in person and was wounded in the leg on the deck of the enemy galley before returning to his own. The Turkish army commander, his shoulder burned by an incendiary grenade, his ship mutilated and his troops half massacred, cut free from the Venetian flagship and tried to retreat. But his galley was taken by another, while Venier, turning his lion's gaze elsewhere, attacked two more enemy ships and sank them both.

Nearby, however, Caterino Malipiero and Giovanni Loredan—surnames steeped in Venetian history—perished in their sinking galleys as the Ottomans advanced. The whole center was now engulfed by a battle

Soldiers from the blood-red galley of Sebastiano Venier (right foreground), the crusty old Venetian commander at the Battle of Lepanto, slash their way onto a rammed Turkish galley, while behind them the Christian flagship of Don Juan of Austria, distinguishable here by its striped mast, grapples with another Turkish ship. Because of their somewhat higher decks and bulwarks, Christian galleys enjoyed a decisive advantage in such boarding encounters: Their soldiers could first bombard the lower Ottoman ships with withering gunfire, and then swarm onto the enemy decks before the Turks could recover.

to the death. The galleys lay meshed together in a graveyard of smoke and splintered oars. In front of the gilded superstructures of their poops, the commanders stood like threatened gods, clutching their weapons or staffs of office, trying to bring order to a chaos that was past human recall. Their huge, unwieldy banners were shredded and holed. Arrows and harquebus balls rattled about their feet. Smoke enveloped the whole sea in a doom-laden twilight, illuminated only by the flash of cannon. At one moment the Turks, fantastical in their sashes and crested turbans, might appear to be in the ascendant, streaming over a galley's sides with a glint of scimitars and a storm of arrows. The next moment the Christians, in waves of darkly glistening steel—close-fitting cuirasses and helmets dashed with plumes—would push inexorably back behind a dinning of muskets and two-handed swords.

The Christian ships poured in cannon shot at point-blank range, and the fire of their musketeers and harquebusiers was so terrible that often it cleared the enemy's fighting decks before a man had boarded. The Spanish musket, weighing some 20 pounds, was particularly lethal. Its two-ounce ball might kill a man 500 yards away and rip through armor and woodwork alike with brute velocity. In the face of this formidable gun, and of the lighter harquebus, the Ottomans often took shelter beneath the rowers' benches. But the Christian boarding parties were mauled in desperate hand-to-hand fighting, whose tumult would mount to a hellish crescendo before fading out into the sobs of the dying. Such assaults were both costly and unpredictable. "In some galleys," wrote an officer, "our men were amazed to find themselves slipping as they boarded, for the enemy had left the gangways open and smeared them with oil, honey and butter."

Soon sinking galleys filled the churning sea with their dead and wounded; and the galley slaves, chained to their oars, drowned in unmourned thousands.

Many in the Christian fleet performed prodigies of valor. A nameless Spaniard, struck in the eye by an arrow, was seen to pull out the shaft with his eye still impaled on it, strap a garter round his head and be the first to board the opposing ship. From the flagship of Genoa, whose captain was struck dead, the 21-year-old Prince of Parma hacked his way through a whole Turkish galley and took it almost singlehandedly.

In the hold of the Sicilian galley *San Giovanni*, a sergeant named Muñoz, lying sick with fever, heard the foot beats of a Turkish boarding party above him. Shouting that there was no longer any need to die of disease, he climbed on deck and led a rush that drove the assailants back through half the ship, killing four. With nine arrow wounds and one leg blown away, he collapsed and died on a rowing bench, shouting to his men: "Each of you do as much."

On the *Real* itself, one of the harquebusiers turned out to be a woman. Called Maria *la Bailadora* (the Dancer), she followed a boarding party onto the *Sultana*, killed a Turk in hand-to-hand combat—and was later rewarded by being allowed to remain in her regiment. Friars and monks were ferocious in the fray. An impatient old Spanish friar tied his crucifix to the end of a halberd and led a boarding party over the side. A Roman Capuchin, seeing his galley being overrun, seized a boat hook and laid about him with it until he had killed seven Turks and driven the rest from the deck.

An even stranger encounter took place when a distant cousin of the Pope, named Ghisliero, led a storming party over the side of a Turkish galley. For years Ghisliero had been a prisoner in Algiers, and he now saw before him an Algerian corsair who had befriended him in his misery. "If you want to save your life," he yelled to the corsair, "jump into the sea." But the man refused to desert his comrades; he flourished his scimitar. Ghisliero, slowly raising his harquebus to his shoulder, shot him through the chest, then, finding him still alive, ended his sufferings with a sword blow.

All this time, while the battle was fading on the Christian left and waxing hot at its center, the southern end of the line, where the Turks heavily outnumbered the Christians, had remained almost silent. Uluch Ali and Doria, each trying to outflank the other, had pushed their vessels farther and farther to the south. Eventually a large gap appeared between the Christians' right and center. Now Uluch Ali turned about. One part of his fleet engaged Doria in a screening attack while he himself, with his heaviest galleys, rowed for the breach in the enemy line to fall on the flank and rear of the Christian center.

There followed some of the bitterest fighting of the battle. The Christians in this part of the line, already exhausted as they turned south to meet the new threat, found themselves assailed on all sides by fresh Muslim forces. The first to suffer the onslaught were the three Maltese ships of the Knights of Saint John, old enemies of the corsairs. Seven Algerian galleys came alongside them and poured in bullets and arrows at close range; then the corsairs boarded the Maltese ships and cut down the last of their depleted crews. The men of the order fought with age-old valor. A Saragossan knight, Gerónimo Ramírez, hacked about him so fearfully that only after he was dead, pierced by countless arrows, did the enemy dare approach him. On board the Maltese flagship the flotilla commander, Prior Pietro Giustiniani, was the last man to fall—pierced by five arrows but captured alive. Among his men, only a Spanish and a Sicilian knight survived, wounded and left for dead among the heaps of the slain.

A mere handful of the knights on the other two ships escaped death, to be taken prisoner. Elaborate funeral rites would be performed later in Florence for one who was thought dead, Borgianni Gianfigliazzi; Gianfigliazzi not only returned from captivity but eventually became Florentine Ambassador in Constantinople. Still more fortunate was a knight named Caraffa, who boarded an enemy *fragata* and was captured there. "While Caraffa was bartering for his life by saying he would fetch a good ransom," wrote an officer of the fleet, "a Neapolitan galley came to the rescue and in an instant (so great are fortune's changes) he had taken his captor captive."

As Uluch Ali's assault continued, Don Alvaro de Bazán, whose reserve squadron was patrolling the Christian rear, saw the danger and sent Cardona to the rescue with eight Sicilian galleys. At once they were encircled by twice their number of Algerian vessels, and a furious fight developed. Uluch Ali himself, who had been towing the captured flagship of the Knights of Saint John out of the battle, realized that he would be overtaken and so cut his prize adrift, leaving the wounded Maltese prior—with 300 Turkish dead cluttering his decks—to fall back into the safety of the Christian hands.

By now the casualties had mounted fearfully on both sides. Whole galleys floated idle and masterless, their soldiers slaughtered, their rowers' corpses at their benches. The papal galley *Florence* lost every knight, soldier and slave, and her captain, Tommaso de Medici, found himself the commander of a mere 16 wounded seamen. The *San Giovanni* drifted like a ghost ship, her company killed to a man, her galley slaves slumped dead at their oars and her captain cut down by two musket balls in the neck.

Meanwhile, in the heart of the Christian line, the battle between the *Sultana* and the *Real* was nearing its climax. Toward 2 o'clock in the afternoon, Don Juan, sword in hand, led an assault party onto the Turkish vessel; at the same time the papal flagship of Colonna, to his right, rowed hard for the *Sultana* and crashed deep into her poop. Between the cross fire of Colonna's harquebusiers and the rush of Spanish steel, Ali Pasha's men fell back. The Ottoman commander himself seems privately to have despaired, for a Spanish historian relates that Ali Pasha, "seeing that there was no hope of any human aid, with his own hands threw into the sea a little casket, said to be of immense value, filled with precious jewels."

Soon afterward, with his Janizaries dying around him, Ali Pasha was killed, reportedly by a harquebus ball that struck him in the forehead. But there are many accounts of his end. One soldier present at the battle wrote that Ali Pasha pulled a knife from his sash, cut his own throat and leaped into the sea. But the most detailed account is that of an Italian officer named Ferrante Caracciolo, who wrote that "after the Turkish flagship had been stormed the soldiers discovered the Pasha lying wounded with a harquebus shot. He said in Italian to some of them: 'Go below. There is money there.' When they realized that this must be the Pasha, a raw Spanish soldier went to kill him; to placate him, the Pasha said: 'Take this chain' (which was very precious); but his words were useless, for without a trace of compassion the man cut off his head and at once jumped into the sea and swam with it to Don Juan, hoping for a handsome reward. But Don Juan answered with displeasure: 'What can I do with that head? Throw it in the sea.' Nevertheless, it was fixed to the stern of his galley on a pike for about an hour."

Within minutes of Ali Pasha's death, the tattered standard of the Koran had been lowered from the masthead of the Sultana and the banner of Christ crucified hoisted in its stead. Don Juan ordered his trumpets to sound, and cries of "Victory! Victory!" spread through the fleet. Everywhere the Turks were being overrun. Thousands surrendered. The sons of Ali Pasha, taken to sea by their father for the first time, were both captured; so was the wily Karakoch. The few Ottoman galleys still resisting in the center were quickly reduced. Their exhausted crews, who had run out of shot and arrows, picked up oranges and lemons and pelted the Christians with them. The Christians, wrote the Venetian Diedo, "out of disdain or ridicule, retaliated by throwing them back at them. This form

Christians in Nuremberg concocted this unlikely portrait of Ali Pasha, the Turkish commander in chief at the Battle of Lepanto, for a broadside printed some nine years after the battle. In the background, his severed head is shown impaled on a pike on his own flagship—a gruesome touch that may be apocryphal, although the Turkish admiral was in fact beheaded and his remains later thrown into the sea.

of conflict seems to have occurred in many places toward the end of the fight, and was a matter for considerable laughter."

Only the Christian right wing was still in commotion, as the Algerians under Uluch Ali fought for survival. Don Alvaro de Bazán and the rest of his reserve were already engaged there—Bazán was wounded twice—and now Don Juan himself, flanked by Venier and Colonna, and with 10 galleys in support, rowed to their aid. Doria had turned back and was attacking Uluch Ali's squadron from the south in a sanguinary revenge. The Venetian galley *Great Christ Risen Again* was boarded and almost overwhelmed by attackers, and her captain killed. But the captain's secretary, rather than see her taken, set fire to the powder magazine and blew ship, attackers and himself to oblivion. Elsewhere a Spanish artillery captain, Federigo Venusta, maimed in the hand by a grenade, ran to one of the oarsmen with a knife, asking him to cut the hand off; but the man fainted. So Venusta cut it off himself, then ran to the galley's hold, thrust the stump into the warm body of a newly killed chicken, had it tied up, and returned to his station.

In the face of such fanaticism, even Uluch Ali's fierce North Africans could make no headway. On one side the Christian center was bearing down unmercifully; on the other, Doria, covered with the blood of a soldier blown to pieces beside him, was clawing at the rear of the Ottoman squadron. Cardona's Sicilian galleys, although outnumbered, had taken or routed the galleys pitted against them. But in the process the Sicilian flagship had been all but devastated—her forecastle and barricades in ruins, her masts a mass of arrows—and Cardona had been mortally wounded in the throat.

Dexterously, painfully, Uluch Ali extracted the remains of his fleet from the conflict. The battle, he knew, was lost. Of his 93-strong squadron a few managed to escape eastward across the gulf to Lepanto, while Uluch Ali himself, with another 13, fled out of the gulf. The rest were captured or sunk. But Uluch Ali took with him the standard of the Knights of Saint John and a single captured Venetian galley. Among the Ottoman commanders he alone survived the battle with honor, and lived robustly on in Constantinople, dying—so it is said—at the age of 90 in the arms of a concubine.

In stunned jubilation the Christian fleet glided over the battlefield in the fading daylight, securing the captured galleys, collecting their wounded and burning the wrecks. The sea had turned to a heaving, blood-tinted desolation, strewn with broken masts and spars, drowned men, barrels and turbans. "The soldiers, sailors and convicts pillaged joyously until nightfall," one Christian later recorded. "There was great booty because of the abundance of gold and silver and rich ornaments that were in the Turkish galleys, especially those of the pashas." That night, as the sky grew overcast, the fleet retreated to a safe anchorage just outside the gulf, leaving the debris to the sea currents, and a few burning hulks to flare alone over the darkening water.

On both sides the casualties had been fearful. Of the Christian fleet only 12 galleys were lost and one captured, but some 7,600 men were killed and an equal number wounded—among them much of the flower of latter-day European chivalry. In these deaths the Venetians suffered

Uluch Ali, the grizzled Algerian corsair who outwitted the Christian right wing at Lepanto, not only survived the battle but prospered because of it, succeeding the slain Ali Pasha as supreme commander of the Ottoman Empire. He went on to harass the Venetians with a brief series of raids in the eastern Mediterranean, but by the time of his death in 1587 the dormant Ottoman navy was wasting away.

Saint Mark, clad in a brown monk's robe, presents Sebastiano Venier for Christ's blessing in an allegorical tribute to the Venetian victors at Lepanto. Commissioned by Venier himself after he was elected Doge, the canvas originally showed a much different scene of a queen (representing Venice) crowning Venier while Saint Mark presided in the firmament. Believing that this implied Venier was a divinely chosen sovereign, the fiercely democratic Senate ordered the picture repainted after he died. Among other changes, a second Venetian soldier (behind Saint Mark) was added to create this generalized memorial.

worst, with more than 4,000 men slain, including 18 galley captains and 12 heads of the city's great houses.

The Muslim losses were far heavier. Up to 30,000 died, including many pashas and governors; some 3,000 Muslims were taken prisoner, and 15,000 Christian galley slaves were liberated from the oars of Ottoman vessels. As for ships, about 240 galleys and galiots were either sunk, burned or captured by the Christians.

Yet Lepanto was a battle without apparent results. Strategically, it bore no fruit at all. Cyprus was not recaptured. That same winter 150 new galleys and eight galleasses were laid down in the shipyards of Constantinople, and when Uluch Ali asked the Grand Vizier how anchors and rigging could be found for such a mighty resurrection, the Vizier merely replied: "The wealth and power of the Empire are of such magnitude that if it were necessary we would make anchors of silver, cables of silk and sails of satin."

Nevertheless, in the intangible half-world of men's hopes and fears, the battle was a turning point. All Christian Europe experienced a surge of relief and self-confidence. For the first time in men's memory, the Turks had been decisively beaten and had proved, as Colonna wrote, to be "no more than other men."

Venice, anxiously awaiting news of the battle, broke into a delirium of joy when on October 17 a galley hove into view trailing captured Turkish banners in the waves and flaunting a crew dressed in Ottoman costumes stripped from the dead. Bells clanged, bonfires blazed, and a prolonged season of pageantry and jubilation ensued. Night after night the shops of the Rialto were alive with light and music; 99 poets celebrated the victory in august (and turgid) verse; commemorative coins were struck; and painters scurried to record the miracle along the ceilings and walls of the Doge's palace.

The battle was seen, above all, as the victory of Christ over mammon. Pope Pius V, placing in Don Juan's debt the whole Christian world, greeted the news with the Biblical verse: "There was a man sent from God, whose name was John."

Within a few years of the Battle of Lepanto, the Mediterranean fell silent. The Ottoman and Spanish Empires, facing each other in the closed arena of the sea, never clashed in such strength again. As the two giants withdrew, it seemed that the empire of Venice, at once so tough and so fragile, must once more assert itself. Yet instead, the sea power of the ancient republic declined, and was never to recover.

With the departure of the great fleets—the Spanish ships to traffic in the wealth of the New World, the Ottoman galleys to rot unused in Constantinople—there began a golden age of piracy. Barbary corsairs, Italian and Dalmatian pirates, intruding Dutch and English, the Knights of Saint John privateering in the name of Christ—all turned their hand against the merchantmen of the republic.

The Venetian galleys and galleasses were ill-suited to combat these predators. Many of the pirates sailed in northern European ships called *bertoni* (Bretons)—three-masted galleons armed with as many as 35 cannon and dauntingly high to board. These sailing vessels were far

Remembrances of victory

To 16th Century Europe the Battle of Lepanto had a significance that far outweighed the immediate concerns of Venetian merchants or Turkish warriors. The Venetian Ambassador to Madrid, Leonardo Donà, conveyed the general feeling when he wrote a jubilant dispatch announcing "the glorious victory that the loving hand of God has given to all Christendom."

Viewed as the culmination of a protracted struggle against the infidel that had begun with the Crusades nearly 500 years before, the victory at Lepanto suggested to Christians that God had once and for all confirmed them in Almighty favor (even though the Turks, declining to share this feeling of finality, continued to press their campaign against Christian Europe for another century and a quarter). Europeans expressed their exultation in virtually every art form —painting and writing, weaving and metalwork, music and architecture. As time went on, they did so in a growing profusion of baroque extravagance and sublime incongruity.

Some of the art was frankly secular; in Spain, King Philip II commanded El Greco to paint his portrait as one of a trio of figures representing the Holy League —Pope Pius V and the Doge of Venice being the other two. And in Rome—100 years after the event—the descendants of fleet commander Marc Antonio Colonna still considered the battle so vital a part of their personal history that they made it the prevailing theme of a set of frescoes they commissioned for their lavish villa.

But nowhere was the artistic expression more fervent than in the Church. On the first anniversary of the battle, Pope Pius V proclaimed the first Sunday in October a religious holiday, and he had commemorative medals struck to remind his flock of quarrelsome nations that, in a dark hour, faith and unity had spared Christians from the terrors of the infidel. Subsequent anniversaries brought similar reminders of the glorious triumph at Lepanto, sustaining the episode in the collective memory of Christian Europe over the next 200 years and more.

On a pulpit carved to resemble a ship in commemoration of the Battle of Lepanto, a gilded Archangel Michael springs to battle from the bowsprit, and cherubs scamper like nimble seamen through rigging of gilded rope. Gracing a monastery chapel in Irsee, Bavaria, the pulpit was built in 1725 at the instigation of the Abbot Willibald Grindl, who as a youth in Austria had seen the Turks turned back from the gates of Vienna in 1683.

An 18th Century plaster relief in a Palermo chapel shows the Virgin Mary—enthroned in the clouds, with Pope Pius V in monk's robes on his knees before her—looking on with approval as Christian and Turkish ships savage each other at Lepanto. Two little urchins perched on a lintel at the bottom of the relief—one clutching a Christian helmet, the other a Turkish turban—add a poignant touch to the scene; they represent the war orphans of Lepanto.

On a monstrance (below)—a vessel used to display a communion wafer— vignettes of the Battle of Lepanto form a meshwork of shimmering gold and silver filigree. An enlarged detail (left) depicts Pope Pius V on the stern of a ship flying Venice's Lion of Saint Mark. Made by Bavarian goldsmith Johann Zeckl, the monstrance was completed in 1708 after 30 years of work.

more maneuverable than Venetian round ships. And the galleasses, useless in rough weather, were too ponderous to catch them. The Venetian light galleys were more successful, but they required constant revictualing and were unable to operate during the winter months. The *bertoni* could not only carry heavier artillery—and fire it broadside instead of from bow and stern—but also required much smaller crews than did galleys and galleasses. So the days of the great war galleys were gone. The huge Spanish Armada that set off to attack England in 1588, just 17 years after Lepanto, included only four galleys and four galleasses among some 130 vessels.

With the discovery of the Americas and the sea route to the Orient, the whole balance of world commerce was inexorably tilting away from Mediterranean states and toward the surging nations of Europe's Atlantic coast: first to Portugal and Spain, then to France, Holland, England. Venetian trade along the Atlantic seaboard disappeared, and in the 1570s tough, seaworthy British *bertoni* penetrated the Mediterranean. As traders, these vessels surpassed the Venetian great galleys. In addition to their smaller crew and ability to sail all year round, they had a larger cargo capacity.

By now Venice itself was relying on foreign vessels for much of its transport. "Foreigners and strangers from remote countries have become masters of all the shipping," ran a report of the Venetian Board of Trade in 1602. "The English in particular, after driving our men from the westward voyage, at present sail the Levantine waters, and voyage to the islands and harbors in our own dominion." By the start of the 17th Century the Dutch, sailing round Africa, had captured the spice trade; and soon afterward the last great outlet of Venetian goods was shut off when the Thirty Years' War devastated Germany.

To counter the *bertoni* sailed by pirates, the Venetians resorted to a neurotic expedient: the building of a monster 240-ton galleon. The vessel inspired frenzied hopes. "The mere rumor that the galleon has put to sea," declared a senator in 1605, "will strike such terror into the hearts of the pirates that they will find it in their own best interests to take to other pursuits."

In this self-blinding belief, the galleon was solemnly blessed and launched in 1608. Her operating cost, at first estimated at 20,000 ducats a year, in fact exceeded 43,000. But her speed was less than hoped, and she was hampered by the slightest contrary wind or hint of calm. If a pirate 20 miles away was to be caught, the wind had to blow strongly behind the galleon all day.

During her 17 months of service, this marine dinosaur, bristling with 76 guns, was at sea almost continuously, escorting merchant shipping. Then technical problems drove her ashore. For two years she stayed in dry dock and was only released, ignominiously, as a merchantman. But on March 24, 1615, as she was about to overwhelm a Tunisian *bertoni* after a two-hour battle, her powder magazine caught fire, and she sank to the bottom in the waters of Cyprus.

By now the republic's once-great Arsenal had declined pitifully. A shortage of raw materials, especially wood, had combined with monetary inflation to deepen its plight. The war galley, with its big complement of manpower, had outgrown its strength. By 1586 there were only 95 galleys left, and for years none had been built. The convict oarsmen received only five ounces of biscuit and one cup of wine a day, and they were pathetically clothed. "Every year," wrote a commander in 1605, "many of the convicts lose their hands or feet as a result of the cold, and at last miserably perish." As for the seamen, a *provveditore* remarked that nobody volunteered for the fleet unless he was a criminal, a half-wit, a debtor or a drunk.

Not only the Arsenal but the city's private shipyards as well lay desolate, and the few remaining vessels were liable to be dismantled for their timber and iron. "The ships of Venice," complained a galleon captain in 1609, "which used—especially the large ones—to be numerous in this city, are now no more." He spoke of the disastrous consequences of buying foreign-built *bertoni* and manning them with foreign officers, more skilled than the Venetians. "And so," he concluded, "as there are no ships built in this city, and as Venetian sailors are not wanted on foreign ships, the old ones go to serve elsewhere and no new ones are trained, so that the seaman's craft is dying out."

The backbone of Venice, in fact, was broken. The seagoing vigor of her elite families of merchants and soldiers had not survived prosperity; instead, they had taken to the mainland, investing in real estate and farming. "Since the noblemen and citizens of Venice had enriched themselves," wrote the diarist Girolamo Priuli, "they wished to enjoy their success and live in the terra firma and elsewhere, devoting themselves to pleasure, delight and the country life, meanwhile abandoning navigation and maritime activities. These were certainly more laborious and troublesome, but it was from the sea that all benefits came."

Originally mounted on the war galley of Doge Francesco Morosini, these matching wooden sculptures of manacled Turks and captured banners and weapons celebrate stunning victories over the Turks in the Peloponnesus and Dalmatia in the 1680s. Despite this brief, renewed demonstration of military prowess, Venice soon yielded dominance of the Adriatic and Levantine trade routes to English and Dutch merchants.

Agriculture continued to flourish after the merchant marine deteriorated. So did some industries, and so, even, did foreign trade—transported in and out of Venice on the ships of others. But by the 18th Century the republic had lost most of its international commercial status. An extravagantly beautiful and gifted city, it was now a port of merely regional importance. During a century of decline Venice's ancient love of the sea became restricted to an innocent senility of galas and pageants along the Grand Canal.

On Ascension Day, 1796, as usual, the Doge and his pampered noblemen were rowed out in the *Bucentaur* for the wedding with the Adriatic. They returned from the ceremony to partake of a banquet that began with Spanish bread, cream, oranges and salted tongue; continued with boiled calf's feet, tripe, pigeons, roast veal and turkey; and ended with custards, cream cheese, asparagus, fennel, artichokes, prunes and dried chestnuts.

But they had little to celebrate. Within three months the armies of Napoleon Bonaparte were camped in the western provinces of the Venetian mainland, and on May 12 of the following year, bludgeoned into surrender by the French and fearing a popular uprising, the Doge and the Great Council of noblemen abdicated their rights and the 1,000-year-old independence of their city-state, never before conquered.

Mobs rampaged through the streets, dreaming of new freedoms, fighting, pillaging. The statues of Prudence and Strength, flanking the Doge's throne, were ripped away, and the gilding was hacked off the *Bucentaur*. Four days later, in the last significant voyage its ships ever made, the Venetian navy transported French troops into the city, carrying its enemy into its own heart over the widowed sea.

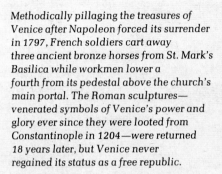

Methodically pillaging the treasures of
Venice after Napoleon forced its surrender
in 1797, French soldiers cart away
three ancient bronze horses from St. Mark's
Basilica while workmen lower a
fourth from its pedestal above the church's
main portal. The Roman sculptures—
venerated symbols of Venice's power and
glory ever since they were looted from
Constantinople in 1204—were returned
18 years later, but Venice never
regained its status as a free republic.

Bibliography

Anderson, R. C.:
Naval Wars in the Levant. Liverpool: Liverpool University Press, 1952.
Oared Fighting Ships. Argus Books, 1976.

Babinger, Franz, *Mehmed the Conqueror and His Time*. Princeton University Press, 1978.

Baedeker, Karl, *Northern Italy*. London: Williams and Norgate, 1868.

Bass, George F., *A History of Seafaring*. London: Thames and Hudson, 1972.

Beck, Marcel, and Franz Babinger, Heinrich Stirnimann, Terukazu Akiyama, "Die Schlacht von Lepanto." *Du* magazine, Vol. 22, May, 1962.

Blair, Claude, *European Armour circa 1066 to circa 1700*. London: B. T. Batsford Ltd., 1958.

Bradford, Ernle, *The Great Betrayal: Constantinople 1204*. London: Hodder and Stoughton, 1967.

Brand, Charles M., *Byzantium Confronts the West 1180-1204*. Harvard University Press, 1968.

Braudel, Fernand, *The Mediterranean and the Mediterranean World in the Age of Philip II*, 2 vols. Harper & Row, 1973.

Brion, Marcel, *Venice: The Masque of Italy*. London: Elek Books, 1962.

Byron, William, *Cervantes: A Biography*. Doubleday, 1978.

Carrero Blanco, Luis, *Lepanto*. Barcelona: Salvat Editores, 1971.

Chambers, D. S., *The Imperial Age of Venice, 1380-1580*. Harcourt Brace Jovanovich, 1970.

Clari, Robert de, *The Conquest of Constantinople*. Transl. by Edgar Holmes McNeal. W. W. Norton, 1964.

Coles, Paul, *The Ottoman Impact on Europe*. Harcourt, Brace & World, 1968.

Darby, H. C., and Harold Fullard, *The New Cambridge Modern History Atlas*. Cambridge: Cambridge University Press, 1970.

Davis, James C., ed. and transl., *Pursuit of Power: Venetian Ambassadors' Reports on Spain, Turkey and France in the Age of Philip II, 1560-1600*. Harper & Row, 1970.

Fabri, Felix, *The Wanderings of Felix Fabri*, Vol. 7. London: Palestine Pilgrims' Text Society, 1897.

Guilmartin, John Francis, Jr., *Gunpowder and Galleys*. Cambridge: Cambridge University Press, 1974.

Hale, J. R., and the Editors of Time-Life Books, *Renaissance* (Great Ages of Man series). Time-Life Books, 1965.

Hale, J. R., ed., *Renaissance Venice*. London: Faber and Faber, 1973.

Hart, Henry H., *Marco Polo: Venetian Adventurer*. University of Oklahoma Press, 1967.

Hazlitt, W. Carew, *The Venetian Republic*. London: Adam and Charles Black, 1900.

Hill, George Francis, *The Frankish Period 1432-1571 (A History of Cyprus*, Vol. 3). Cambridge: Cambridge University Press, 1948.

Humble, Richard, *Marco Polo*. G. P. Putnam's Sons, 1975.

Hussey, J. M., *The Byzantine World*. Harper & Brothers, 1961.

Inalcik, Halil, *The Ottoman Empire: The Classical Age, 1300-1600*. Transl. by Norman Itzkowitz and Colin Imber. Praeger Publishers, 1973.

Joinville, Jean de, and Geoffroy de Villehardouin, *Chronicles of the Crusades*. Transl. by M.R.B. Shaw. London: Penguin Books, 1963.

Kemp, Peter, ed., *The Oxford Companion to Ships and the Sea*. London: Oxford University Press, 1976.

Kinross, Lord, *The Ottoman Centuries: The Rise and Fall of the Turkish Empire*. William Morrow, 1977.

Landström, Björn, *The Ship*. Transl. by Michael Phillips. Doubleday, 1961.

Lane, Frederic C.:
Andrea Barbarigo, Merchant of Venice 1418-1449. Johns Hopkins University Press, 1944.
Venetian Ships and Shipbuilders of the Renaissance. Johns Hopkins University Press, 1934.
Venice: A Maritime Republic. Johns Hopkins University Press, 1973.

Lane-Poole, Stanley, *The Barbary Corsairs*. G. P. Putnam's Sons, 1901.

Lloyd, Christopher, *Atlas of Maritime History*. Arco Publishing, 1975.

Longworth, Philip, *The Rise and Fall of Venice*. London: Constable, 1974.

Lorenzetti, Giulio, *Venice and Its Lagoons*, Historical-artistic guide. Rome: Istituto Poligrafico Dello Stato, 1961.

McNeill, William H., *Venice, the Hinge of Europe, 1081-1797*. University of Chicago Press, 1974.

Malipiero, Domenico, *Annali Veneti, dall'anno 1457 al 1500*. Florence: Gio. Pietro Vieusseux, Direttore-Editore, 1844.

Molmenti, Pompeo, *Venice: Its Individual Growth from the Earliest Beginnings to the Fall of the Republic*, Parts 1 and 2. London: John Murray, 1907.

Mondadori, Arnoldo, ed., *Cervantes: His Life, His Times, His Works*. Transl. by Salvator Attansio. American Heritage, 1970.

Muir, Edward, "Images of Power: Art and Pageantry in Renaissance Venice." *The American Historical Review*, Vol. 84, February, 1979.

Newett, Margaret M., *Canon Pietro Casola's Pilgrimage to Jerusalem*. Manchester: University of Manchester Publications, 1907.

Norwich, John Julius, *Venice: The Rise to Empire*. London: Allen Lane, 1977.

Palmer, R. R., and Joel Colton, *A History of the Modern World*. Alfred A. Knopf, 1950.

Petrie, Charles, *Don John of Austria*. W. W. Norton, 1967.

Prescott, H.F.M., *Friar Felix at Large*. Greenwood Press, 1950.

Priuli, Girolamo, *I Diarii 1494-1512*. Bologna: Nicola Zanichelli. N.D.

Pullan, Brian, ed., *Crisis and Change in the Venetian Economy in the Sixteenth and Seventeenth Centuries*. London: Methuen, 1968.

Queller, Donald E., *The Fourth Crusade: The Conquest of Constantinople, 1201-1204*. University of Pennsylvania Press, 1977.

Ragg, Laura M., *Crises in Venetian History*. London: Methuen, 1928.

Rubin de Cervin, G. B., *Bateaux et Batellerie de Venise*. Paris: Edita Lausanne, 1978.

Runciman, Steven, *A History of the Crusades*, Vols. 1-3. Cambridge: Cambridge University Press, 1951-1954.

Sanuto, Marino, *I. Diarii*. Venice: A Spese Degli Editori, 1879.

Setton, Kenneth M., editor-in-chief, *A History of the Crusades:*
Vol. 1, *The First Hundred Years*. Ed. by Marshall W. Baldwin. University of Wisconsin Press, 1969.
Vol. 2, *The Later Crusades, 1189-1311*. Ed. by Robert Lee Wolff and Harry W. Hazard. University of Pennsylvania Press, 1962.

Shaw, Stanford, *History of the Ottoman Empire and Modern Turkey*, Vol. 1. Cambridge: Cambridge University Press, 1976.

Stirling-Maxwell, William, *Don John of Austria*. 2 vols. London: Longmans, Green, 1883.

Tenenti, Alberto, *Piracy and the Decline of Venice 1580-1615*. Transl. by Janet and Brian Pullan. University of California Press, 1967.

Warner, Oliver, *Great Sea Battles*. Spring Books, 1968.

Wiel, Alethea, *The Navy of Venice*. London: John Murray, 1910.

William, Archbishop of Tyre, *A History of Deeds Done Beyond the Sea*. Transl. by Emily Atwater Babcock and A. C. Krey. 2 vols. Columbia University Press, 1943.

Acknowledgments

The index for this book was prepared by Gale Linck Partoyan. For their help in the preparation of this book, the editors wish to thank the following: John Batchelor, artist, and John Francis Guilmartin Jr. and Frederic Chapin Lane, consultants (pages 92-94); Bill Hezlep, artist, and John Francis Guilmartin Jr., consultant (maps, pages 53, 143, 147-149); Peter McGinn, artist (ships, pages 147-149, and endpaper maps); Lloyd K. Townsend, artist, and Frederic Chapin Lane, Edward Muir and Professor Guido Perocco, consultants (pages 70-71).

The editors also wish to thank: In Belgium: Brussels—Lucien Basch; Bibliothèque Royale Albert; Bruges—Stedelijk Museum. In France: Paris—François Avril, Curator, Bibliothèque Nationale; Sylvie Béguin, Curator, Dominique Thiébaut, Curator, Musée du Louvre; Hervé Cras, Director of Historical Studies, Denise Chaussegroux, Researcher, Marjolaine Mathikine, Librarian, Musée de la Marine; Rueil-Malmaison—Yvan David, Curator, Musée de la Malmaison. In Germany: Irsee—Alfred Schorer. In Italy: Venice—Maria Francesca Tiepolo, Director, Archivio di Stato; Professor Gian Albino Ravalli Modoni, Director, Mario Favaretto, Biblioteca Nazionale Marciana; Giovanna Scire' Nepi, Director, Galleria dell' Accademia; Professor Guido Perocco, Director, Museo d'Arte Moderna; Professor Giandomenico Romanelli, Director, Lucia Casanova, Superintendent, Mario de Fina, Museo Correr; Giambattista Rubin de Cervin, Director, Carlo Ramelli, Museo Storico Navale; Umberto Franzoi, Director, Silvano Boldrin, Ireneo Manoli, Sergio Brussa, Palazzo Ducale; Giacomo Fioretti, Ufficio Tecnico, Procuratoria di San Marco; Professor Francesco Valcanover, Superintendent, Soprintendenza ai Beni Artistici e Storici di Venezia. In Spain: Madrid—Armería Real, Palacio Real; Don Fernando Fuertes de Villavicencio, Consejero Delegado Gerente, Don Manuel Dávila Jalón, Inspector General de Museos, Patrimonio Nacional. In Turkey: Istanbul—Sabahattin Batur, Curator, Gengiz Köseoglu, Filiz Çagman, Topkapi Sarayi Muzesi. In the United Kingdom: London—Admiral Sir Charles Madden, B.T., G.C.B., D.L. In the United States: Washington, D.C.—Gary Vikan, Associate Curator, Virgil Crisafulli, Byzantine Research Library, Dumbarton Oaks; Dr. Esin Atil, Curator of Islamic Art, Freer Gallery of Art; Arlington, Virginia—Vita Iocco; Charlottesville, Virginia—Professor Ernest B. Gilman, Department of English, University of Virginia; Chicago, Illinois—Professor Halil Inalcik, Department of History, University of Chicago; College Station, Texas—Richard Steffy, Institute of Nautical Archaeology; New Haven, Connecticut—Marjorie Wynne, Research Librarian, Beinecke Rare Book and Manuscript Library, Yale University; Oxon Hill, Maryland—Karin Kinney; Princeton, New Jersey—Professor Donald E. Queller, Institute for Advanced Studies; Rochester, New York—Dr. Harry Hazard; Whitehall, Virginia—Susan Bryan. In Yugoslavia: Biograd na moru—Branka Yuraga, Director, Zavičajni Muzej; Zadar—Professor Ivo Petricioli, Filozofski Fakultet; Sofija Petricioli, Narodnog Muzej.

The map showing Venetian merchant galley fleets is based on the map on page 341 of Venice: A Maritime Republic, by Frederic C. Lane, © 1973, and was redrawn by permission of the publisher, The Johns Hopkins University Press.

Charts of the Battle of Lepanto are based on © Luis Carrero Blanco and Salvat Editores, 1971, by permission of the publisher.

Picture Credits

Credits from left to right are separated by semicolons, from top to bottom by dashes.
Cover: Mirko Toso, courtesy Museo Correr, Venice. Front and back endpapers: Drawing by Peter McGinn.
Page 3: Erich Lessing, courtesy Museo Correr, Venice. 6, 7: Erich Lessing, courtesy Biblioteca Nazionale Marciana, Venice. 9: Beinecke Rare Book and Manuscript Library, Yale University. 10, 11: Galleria dell' Accademia, Venice; by permission of the Trustees of the British Museum. 13: Photo Bibliothèque Nationale, Paris. 15: Jean Roubier, Paris, courtesy Rheims Cathedral. 16, 17: Erich Lessing, courtesy Palazzo Ducale, Venice. 20: Museo Correr, Venice. 22, 25: Erich Lessing, courtesy Palazzo Ducale, Venice. 28: Photo Bibliothèque Nationale, Paris. 31: By permission of the British Library. 33: Biblioteca Apostolica Vaticana, Rome. 34: Giorgio Biserni, courtesy S. Giovanni Evangelista, Ravenna—Alinari, courtesy S. Giovanni Evangelista, Ravenna. 36, 37: Erich Lessing, courtesy Palazzo Ducale, Venice. 38, 39: Erich Lessing, courtesy Basilica San Marco, Venice; Erich Lessing, courtesy Tesoro di San Marco, Venice. 40, 41: Scala, courtesy Tesoro di San Marco, Venice—Fabbri, courtesy Tesoro di San Marco, Venice; Scala, courtesy Tesoro di San Marco, Venice. 42, 43: Fulvio Roiter, courtesy Basilica San Marco, Venice; inset, Erich Lessing, courtesy Basilica San Marco, Venice. 44: Erich Lessing, courtesy Galleria dell' Accademia, Venice. 46, 47: Erich Lessing, courtesy Palazzo Ducale, Venice. 49: Erich Lessing, courtesy Museo Correr, Venice. 50, 51: Erich Lessing, courtesy Galleria dell' Accademia, Venice. 53: Map by Bill Hezlep. 54: Erich Lessing, courtesy Palazzo Ducale, Venice. 57-60: David Lees, courtesy Zavičajni Muzej, Biograd na moru, Yugoslavia. 62: Beinecke Rare Book and Manuscript Library, Yale University. 63: Erich Lessing, courtesy Museo Correr, Venice. 64: The Bodleian Library, Oxford, Roll 161C. 66, 67: Mirko Toso, courtesy Biblioteca Nazionale Marciana, Venice. 68: Photo Bibliothèque Nationale, Paris. 70-77: Drawings by Lloyd K. Townsend. 78, 79: Scala, courtesy Museo Correr, Venice. 82, 83: Mirko Toso, courtesy Museo Correr, Venice. 84, 85: Erich Lessing, courtesy Museo Correr, Venice. 87: Alinari, courtesy San Eustorgio, Milan—Museo Storico Navale, Venice. 88, 89: Bohm, courtesy Basilica San Marco, Venice; Alinari, courtesy Basilica San Marco, Venice. 90: Mirko Toso, courtesy Museo Correr, Venice. 92-94: Drawings by John Batchelor. 96, 97: Museo Correr, Venice. 98: G. Mazetto, courtesy Museo Storico Navale, Venice. 100: Reproduced by courtesy of the Trustees, The National Gallery, London. 102: Ara Güler, courtesy Topkapi Sarayi Muzesi, Istanbul. 105: Lauros-Giraudon, courtesy Musée du Louvre, Paris. 107: Topkapi Sarayi Muzesi, Istanbul. 110, 111: By permission of the Trustees of the British Museum. 113: Fondazione Giorgio Cini, Venice. 114: Ara Güler, courtesy Topkapi Sarayi Muzesi, Istanbul. 117: The Metropolitan Museum of Art, gift of William H. Riggs, 1913; Derek Bayes, from the Collection of The Tower of London. 118, 119: Robert Royal, courtesy Royal Armory, Palacio Real, Madrid; Erich Lessing, courtesy Palazzo Ducale, Venice (2)—Robert Royal, courtesy Royal Armory, Palacio Real, Madrid (2). 120: Scala, courtesy Palazzo Du-

Index

Printed in U.S.A.